iPad® 2
QuickSteps™

About the Author

Joli Ballew is an award-winning, best-selling technical author of 40+ books. Joli has been working with computers, gadgets, and all things media since her freshman year in college in 1982, when she majored in computer science and system analysis, ultimately ending up with a degree in mathematics. Joli has written several books related to phones and mobile technologies, including the extremely popular *How to Do Everything: iPad* (McGraw-Hill) and *How to Do Everything: BlackBerry Storm2* (McGraw-Hill). Joli also teaches computer classes at various colleges in the Dallas area, and manages several websites.

Beyond writing books and teaching classes, Joli is a Microsoft MVP and holds multiple Microsoft certifications, studies new technologies regularly, and attends both the Consumer Electronics Show and the Microsoft MVP Summit every year in order to keep up with the latest and greatest technologies. In her spare time, Joli exercises at her local gym, works outside tending to her manicured lawn, and serves as the butler for her two cats, Pico and Lucy, and their pet gerbil, George.

You can contact Joli and post questions through her iPad Facebook page, How To Do Everything: iPad. If you don't use Facebook, Joli welcomes your correspondence via e-mail at Joli_Ballew@hotmail.com.

About the Technical Editor

Donald Bell is a senior editor for CNET.com, covering portable media players and tablets. He is the writer responsible for CNET's official iPad review, and he regularly publishes tutorials for CNET's iPad Atlas blog. You can also hear him each week on CNET's Crave podcast. When he's not testing the latest gadgets, he enjoys playing guitar, listening to old records, and being a dad.

iPad® 2
QuickSteps™

JOLI BALLEW

New York Chicago San Francisco
Lisbon London Madrid Mexico City
Milan New Delhi San Juan
Seoul Singapore Sydney Toronto

The McGraw·Hill Companies

Cataloging-in-Publication Data is on file with the Library of Congress

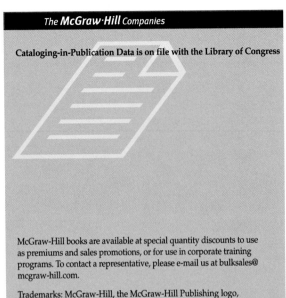

iPad® 2 QUICKSTEPS™

1234567890 QDB QDB 10987654321

ISBN   978-0-07-177427-7
MHID   0-07-177427-0

SPONSORING EDITOR / Megg Morin

EDITORIAL SUPERVISOR / Jody McKenzie

PROJECT MANAGER / Tania Andrabi, Cenveo Publisher Services

ACQUISITIONS COORDINATOR / Joya Anthony

TECHNICAL EDITOR / Donald Bell

COPY EDITOR / Lisa McCoy

PROOFREADER / Paul Tyler

INDEXER / Claire Splan

PRODUCTION SUPERVISOR / George Anderson

COMPOSITION / Cenveo Publisher Services

ILLUSTRATION / Cenveo Publisher Services

ART DIRECTOR, COVER / Jeff Weeks

COVER DESIGNER / Pattie Lee

SERIES CREATORS / Marty and Carole Matthews

SERIES DESIGN / Bailey Cunningham

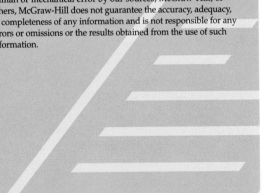

For my family, Dad, Jennifer, Cosmo, and Andrew; thanks for all you do!

Contents at a Glance

Contents

Chapter 3   Communicating with Mail 37

Chapter 4   Using the Camera, Displaying Photos,
Viewing Videos, and Exploring FaceTime 53

Acknowledgments

This book is a team effort of truly talented people.

The Cast:

Megg Morin, sponsoring editor, project editor, friend, and iPad enthusiast. Megg hired me once again to write another iPad book and kept everyone in line, on track, and on time. Megg was always available, which is very important when pushing a book out quickly.

Donald Bell, technical editor, who meticulously read and corrected my work, and did so quickly and precisely.

Tania Andrabi, project manager, who coordinated the copyediting, proofreading, and layout and made sure all the right details got to the right spots.

Jody McKenzie, editorial supervisor, and **George Anderson**, production supervisor, who provided additional support where needed to help make the production process run smoothly.

Neil Salkind, my agent, who goes out of his way to keep me busy. He's a great friend and my biggest fan. I'm sure I wouldn't be where I am today without him.

My family, who supports my work and understands the ups and downs of a writer's life!

Introduction

QuickSteps™ books are recipe books for computer users. They answer the question "How do I…?" by providing quick sets of steps to accomplish the most common tasks in a particular program. The sets of steps are the central focus of the book. QuickSteps sidebars show you how to quickly do many small functions or tasks that support the primary functions. Notes, Tips, and Cautions augment the steps, yet they are presented in such a manner as to not interrupt the flow of the steps. The brief introductions are minimal rather than narrative, and numerous illustrations and figures, many with callouts, support the steps.

QuickSteps™ books are organized by function and the tasks needed to perform that function. Each function is a chapter. Each task, or "How To," contains the steps needed for accomplishing the function along with relevant Notes, Tips, Cautions, and screenshots. Tasks will be easy to find through:

- The table of contents, which lists the functional areas (chapters) and tasks in the order they are presented

- A How-To list of tasks on the opening page of each chapter

- The index with its alphabetical list of terms used in describing the functions and tasks

- Color-coded tabs for each chapter or functional area with an index to the tabs just before the table of contents

Conventions Used in This Book

iPad® 2 QuickSteps™ uses several conventions designed to make the book easier for you to follow:

- A ⊙ or a ⊘ in the table of contents or the How To list in each chapter references a QuickSteps or a QuickFacts sidebar in a chapter.

- **Bold type** is used for words on the screen that you are to do something with, such as click **Save As** or open **File**.

- *Italic type* is used for a word or phrase that is being defined or otherwise deserves special emphasis.

- <u>Underlined type</u> is used for text that you are to type from the keyboard.

- When you see the command, **CTRL/CMD**, you are to press the **CTRL** key in Windows or the **CMD** key on the Mac; **ALT/OPT**, press the **ALT** key in Windows or the **OPTIONS** key on the Mac.

- SMALL CAPITAL LETTERS are used for keys on the keyboard such as **ENTER** and **SHIFT**.

- When you are expected to enter a command, you are told to press the key(s). If you are to enter text or numbers, you are told to type them. Specific letters or numbers to be entered will be underlined.

- When you are to click the mouse button on a screen command or menu, you will be told to "Click **File | Open**" which means, "Click **File** and then click **Open**."

How to...

Chapter 1
Getting Started

An iPad is a tablet computer designed, developed, and available from Apple that enables you to access the Internet, read e-books, upload and view pictures, watch movies, play games, and more from just about anywhere and at any time. It comes with its own apps like Calendar, Contacts, Safari, Notes, Maps, Photos, FaceTime, Photo Booth, Mail, and others, and you can obtain additional apps through the included App Store.

This chapter explains how to activate, set up, personalize, and protect your iPad so that you can use it and get the most from it right from the start. If you have a Wi-Fi + 3G iPad, you'll also learn a little about choosing a data plan so you can have always-available Internet access.

Figure 1-1: *It's best to accept the defaults during the installation of iTunes.*

Activate and Explore Your iPad

You have to activate your iPad before you can use it. You perform the activation tasks by connecting your iPad to a computer. Make sure to choose the computer you use most at home or at work, because the computer you choose at this time is the one you'll use to manage your iPad from now on. (You should only sync your iPad with one computer at a time; if you try to sync with more than one, data loss can occur.) You need to install the latest version of Apple's free iTunes software on the computer you select before you start to simplify the process (although you can certainly connect first and install iTunes second).

Install iTunes

You need iTunes to activate your iPad and to manage and sync data between your computer and your iPad. Some things you may opt to sync are your media (including music, videos, movies, pictures, music videos, TV shows, podcasts, etc.), and contacts, calendar appointments, and other data. You'll also use iTunes to back up and restore your iPad.

To download, install, and set up iTunes and obtain an iTunes Store account on a Windows-based PC (the steps for a Mac are similar but not exactly the same):

1. From your computer, click the **Internet Explorer** icon on the taskbar.

2. Navigate to www.itunes.com/download.

3. Verify that you want to leave the two options selected to receive e-mail notifications from Apple (and input your e-mail address if so); if you do not want to receive e-mail from Apple, deselect these items.

4. Click **Download Now**.

5. Click **Run**, and when the download has completed, click **Run** again.

6. Click **Next**.

7. Click **I Accept The Terms In This License Agreement**, and click **Next**.

8. Accept the defaults and click **Install** (see Figure 1-1).

9. Leave **Open iTunes After The Installer Exits** selected. Click **Finish**.

NOTE

Your iPad's battery should have shipped fully charged or at least charged enough to get started. However, you may have to charge the battery if it's depleted that charge.

TIP

If you already have iTunes installed on your computer, open it. If you're on a Windows PC, click **Help** and click **Check For Updates**. For Mac users, click the **iTunes** menu and click **Check For Updates**.

With iTunes installed, you're ready to connect your iPad. Once connected, you'll be prompted to work through the activation process in a specific order, which involves creating an iTunes Store account and registering your iPad. To perform these tasks you must have access to the Internet, a way to pay for iTunes Store purchases (using a credit card or PayPal), and the included Universal Serial Bus (USB) cable and available USB port on your computer.

Register Your iPad

To register your iPad and to create a new iTunes Store account (Apple ID):

1. With iTunes open, connect your iPad to your computer using the supplied USB cable.

2. With your iPad connected to your computer, at the iTunes Welcome page, click **Continue**.

3. Select **I Have Read And Agree To The iPad Software License Agreement**, and click **Continue**.

4. On the iTunes Account (Apple ID) page, either log in with an existing Apple ID or select **I Do Not Have An Apple ID**. Click **Continue**.

5. If you do not have an Apple ID, work through the steps to create one. You'll also have to provide a form of payment for future purchases. Click **Continue** when finished.

6. At the Register Your iPad page, fill in the required information. Click **Submit** when finished.

7. If prompted to try MobileMe, click **Not Now**.

8. On the Set Up iPad page, type a name for your iPad. On that same page deselect the three syncing options. You'll learn to set up syncing in the next section, and you can choose then exactly what you want to sync and what you do not.

9. Click **Done**.

10. Your first sync will begin. If you've not selected anything to sync, it won't take long for the process to complete (see Figure 1-2).

11. Leave iTunes open and your iPad connected for now.

*Figure 1-2: **Because you opted not to sync anything yet, the syncing process won't take long.***

```
                              iTunes
              Syncing "Joli's iPad"
                     Finishing sync
       ▄▄▄▄▄▄▄▄▄▄▄▄▄▄▄▄▄▄▄▄▄▄▄▄▄▄▄▄▄
     Summary   Info   Apps   Music   Movies   TV Shows   Podcasts   iT
```

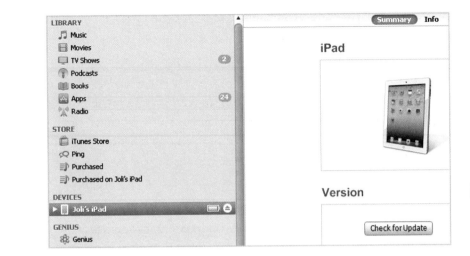

To make sure you have the latest software on your iPad, in iTunes on your computer:

1. Select your iPad in the left pane.
2. Click the **Summary** tab in the right pane.
3. Click **Check For Update** or **Update**.
4. If an update is available, install it.
5. Leave iTunes open and your iPad connected for now.

Explore What Can Be Synced

You can sync almost any kind of data imaginable. You'll want to start by syncing music, movies, and photos, most likely. You may also keep calendars, bookmarks, and contacts on your computer that you'd also like to have access to on your iPad. You sync this information by selecting it in iTunes. Here are a few of the tabs in iTunes you'll want to explore now, and the Apply option which makes syncing for the data you've chosen to occur immediately.

INFO

Click the **Info** tab to sync contacts, calendars, mail accounts (minus your passwords), bookmarks, and notes. No matter what you opt to sync, if you make changes on one device, during the next sync, changes will be copied to the other.

When you sync contacts, you get to choose from where to obtain the data, based on the contact information stored on your computer. There is likely no way to fill up your iPad with this information, even if you opted to sync each option.

You'll choose to sync mail if you don't want to set up your e-mail accounts on your iPad manually but would instead rather copy (sync) the information from your computer. You sync bookmarks to keep Internet Explorer Favorites or Safari Bookmarks on your computer synced with the bookmarks on your iPad. Sync notes to copy notes you create on your iPad to your computer and vice

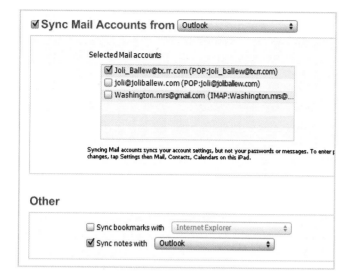

versa, provided you have a compatible notes program on your desktop computer.

MUSIC

Click the **Music** tab to sync all music or only specific artists, playlists, genres, or albums. You can also opt to sync music videos, voice notes, or to automatically fill free space on your iPad with songs. To see how much space your entire music library would require of your iPad, click **Entire Music Library**, and look at the **Capacity** bar that runs across the bottom of the screen (see Figure 1-3).

MOVIES

Click the **Movies** tab to see what, if any, movies on your computer can be synced to your iPad. If you have quite a few movies on your computer,

Figure 1-3: **Use the Music tab to select what music to sync and to see how much space your entire music library would require.**

you probably can't sync them all because you won't have enough room on your iPad to store them. Click **Sync Movies**, but do not select Automatically Include. Then, select only the movies you want to sync to your iPad.

PHOTOS

Click the **Photos** tab to sync photos. Click **Sync Photos From** to see how much space syncing all photos in a specific folder will consume on your iPad. Since some videos also appear in various picture folders on your computer, select **Include Videos** if desired. It's likely that you can sync all of your photos provided you leave Include Videos deselected.

APPLY

After you've selected a bit of data to sync (copy) to your iPad, click **Apply**. The sync will occur, and the selected data will be copied to your iPad.

NOTE

Other tabs are available in iTunes, and some will appear only after you've obtained a specific type of data. As you acquire data, look for these tabs, including iTunes U, TV Shows, and Books.

If, during the setup processes, you opted to sync some data to your iPad, as introduced in the "Configuring iTunes" QuickSteps and the "Understanding Sync Options" QuickFacts, you will have to wait until syncing completes to access the Home screen. If you use the slider while a sync is in progress, the sync will cancel. However, the next time you connect your iPad, the sync process will continue. It's best to wait while the sync process completes. You'll see the progress of the iPad sync from both the iPad Home screen and iTunes (shown here).

QUICKSTEPS

CONFIGURING iTUNES

You'll learn about syncing throughout this book in various chapters and in Chapter 10; however, you will want to sync some things now to get some data on your iPad. You sync data using iTunes while your iPad is connected to your computer. With iTunes open and your iPad connected, look at each of the tabs and consider the options. If you're comfortable doing so, select some data now to sync and click Apply; if you aren't yet ready, you can wait for specific instructions on selecting data later in the book. You're safe selecting some photos and some music; you can't go wrong there.

UNDERSTANDING SYNC OPTIONS

You can sync entire libraries or you can handpick the data to sync from your computer to your iPad.

SYNC ENTIRE MEDIA LIBRARIES

iTunes offers the option to sync all music, all photos, all videos, all books, all podcasts, all apps, and/or all other types of media. This isn't always optimal, though, because you will generally have much more data on your computer than your iPad can store. Thus, you'll often opt to sync only selected media.

SYNC SELECTED MEDIA

Opt to sync only media you handpick, such as your favorite music or playlists, a folder of your most precious photos, one or two videos you've yet to see, and podcasts and audio books you've yet to listen to. This enables you to swap in and out media as desired while at the same time managing how much media is stored on your iPad.

The iPad is only meant to be associated with one computer at a time. Plugging the iPad into a different computer than the one used for setup (and opting to sync to it) could result in loss of data.

After any syncing has completed, you'll have access to the iPad Home screen (you'll need to use the slider to unlock the iPad first). This is the ultimate goal of setting up your iPad, of course, and once you're here you have completed the required setup tasks. Figure 1-4 shows the iPad Home screen and how it will likely appear when you first access it. Familiarize yourself with the parts of the screen now, and you'll be better able to follow along in this book.

Explore the Outside of the iPad

Now that you're all set up and synced, let's look at the outside of the iPad. Several buttons and connections are available. There's a 30-pin docking port that allows you to charge your iPad or connect it to your computer, located just under the Home button; a stereo headphone mini-jack; a switch to mute the volume or lock the screen rotation; and more. The list here is complete; while reading through it, locate each of these on your own iPad.

Carefully turn your iPad in all directions and look for the following ports and features:

- **Home button**   The small, round button on the front of the iPad near the bottom. Use it to access the Lock screen when the iPad is inactive, to access the Home screen when the iPad is in use, and to perform other tasks outlined in this book.

- **30-pin dock connector**   The dock connector is located on the bottom of the iPad. This is where you connect accessories, such as the battery charger, docking stations, the Apple Camera Connection Kit (optional), and other devices.

- **Built-in speaker**   The speaker is located at the bottom of the iPad when holding the iPad in Portrait mode, under the Home button, on the right side.

- **3.5 mm stereo headphone mini-jack**   A standard headphone jack that accepts generic headphones and headsets is located at the top of the iPad on the left.

- **Microphone**   The pinhole microphone is located on the top of the iPad, in the center, just above the front-facing camera lens.

- **Silent/Screen Rotation Lock**   This lock is located on the right side of the iPad near the top, just above the volume buttons. Slide this switch to silence the iPad or to apply the Screen Rotation Lock. What happens when you use this switch depends on how it's configured in Settings (which you'll learn how to change later in this book). By default,

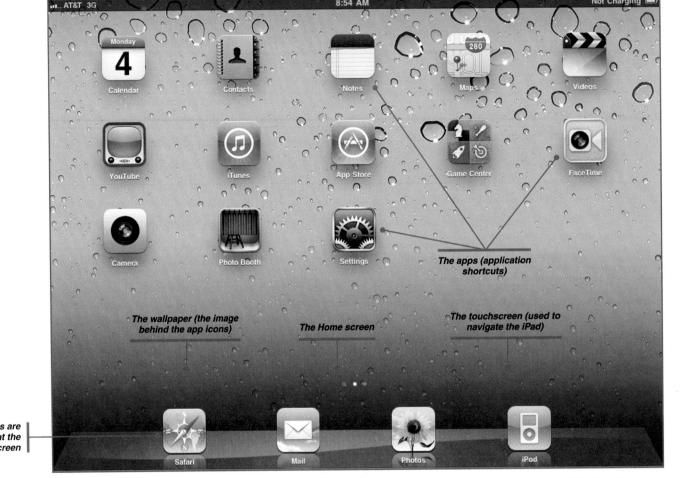

Some apps are available at the bottom of the screen

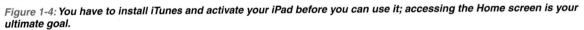

Figure 1-4: *You have to install iTunes and activate your iPad before you can use it; accessing the Home screen is your ultimate goal.*

the switch is set to silence the iPad. If you want to leave the setting as Mute, but still want quick access to locking the screen's rotation, you can double-tap the **Home** button, flick from left to right at the bottom of the page, and tap the **Lock Orientation** option.

- **Volume** The volume buttons are located on the right side of the iPad underneath the Silent/Screen Rotation Lock.

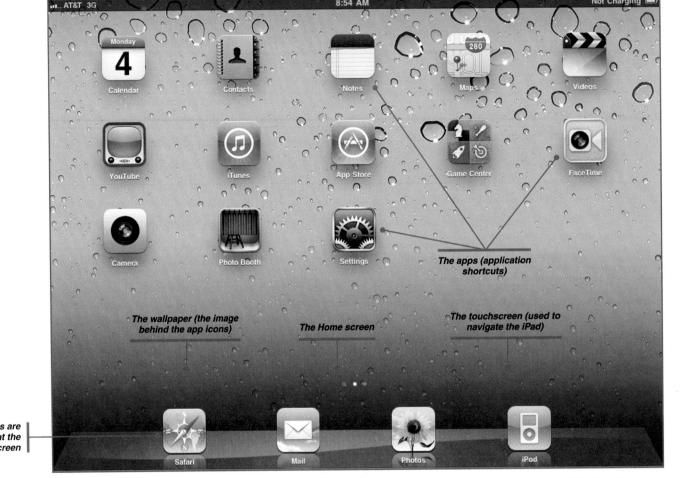

NOTE

There are lots of things you can't see, including the accelerometer that enables you to turn your iPad in various directions and have games and apps respond to your movements, built-in wireless and possibly 3G capabilities, and built-in Bluetooth capabilities. There's also a battery and physical storage, among other things.

- **Sleep/Wake and On/Off**   The Sleep/Wake button is located on the top of the iPad on the right; just apply a short press. You can use this button to turn off and on the iPad as well; apply a long press and hold, and then opt to turn off the iPad when prompted.

- **Camera lenses**   The front- and rear-facing camera lenses are at the top of their respective sides of the iPad.

- **Micro-SIM card tray**   Located at the top, on the left side, and available only on the AT&T Wi-Fi + 3G models. You'll need a SIM eject tool (or a paperclip) to gain access.

Explore the Home Screen

The Lock screen is what you see when you turn on or access your iPad after it's been asleep or turned off (or when you stop playing a Picture Frame slideshow). This is a safeguard to keep it from being inadvertently enabled when not in use. Once you've used the slider to access the iPad, what you see is the Home screen. The Home screen was detailed earlier in Figure 1-4. This screen gives you one-tap access to everything that's available on it. Later in this chapter you'll learn how to personalize this screen by moving the icons, and how to add or remove icons to make the iPad uniquely yours. For now, you'll want to explore what's on the Home screen already and learn to navigate around in it. The Home screen icons you'll want to familiarize yourself with are shown in Figure 1-5.

Figure 1-5: The iPad's Home screen offers one-tap access to the apps on it.

The icons you'll see on the Home screen when you first turn it on include

- **Calendar**   A fully functional calendar that allows you to create and manage events; configure reminders for events; view the calendar by day, month, and lists of events; and incorporate new calendars by syncing them from your computer.

- **Contacts**   This is an application you use to manage the contacts you sync or add manually. You can easily add new contacts or edit existing ones, select a contact to communicate with, or share contact information with others.

- **Notes**   This application allows you to take notes easily. The Notes app looks like a yellow, lined steno pad and allows you to create notes with a virtual keyboard and then e-mail them, delete them, or save them for future reference.

- **Maps**   A full-fledged application for getting directions to local restaurants or points of interest; a contact's physical address; your current position; and for showing traffic, satellite views, typed directions, and more.

- **Videos**   An option for managing the videos you own and watching videos you get from iTunes.

- **YouTube**   This application allows you to quickly view YouTube video content, watch the most popular videos of the day, and search for videos you want to view. With YouTube, you can also mark your favorite videos so you can access them later or view similar videos easily. This is an app, however, and doesn't take you to the actual website.

- **iTunes**   This application allows you to preview and purchase music and media on your iPad. (As with some of the other apps, you need to be online to access the iTunes Store.) Note that the iTunes app on the iPad is only a storefront and does not handle media management and playback like iTunes on a computer does.

- **App Store**   The App Store is where you purchase and download apps, including those that enable you to engage in social networking, manage your finances, obtain additional information about products you plan to buy, play games, share data, and more. Think of anything you'd like to do with your iPad; there's likely an app for that!

- **Game Center**   The Game Center makes it easy to find games, play games, and add gaming friends. You can create an online gaming identity and keep track of the games you play and the scores you earn, among other things.

- **FaceTime**   FaceTime lets you hold video conversations with anyone else using an iPad 2, iPhone 4, new iPod touch, or Mac over Wi-Fi. It works just as you'd expect a "video phone" to work, by assisting you in placing a call to a contact, initiating and holding a video conversation, and hanging up when your call is complete.

- **Camera** The Camera app offers access to the front- and rear-facing cameras, enabling you to take both photos and video (and hold FaceTime conversations).

- **Photo Booth** Photo Booth can be used to take pictures and apply effects to those pictures.

- **Settings** This application enables you to turn on and off Wi-Fi; change sounds, brightness, and wallpaper; configure e-mail, contacts, and calendar options; change Safari defaults; change iPod defaults; and more.

There are also four icons located across the bottom of the screen, in an area called the Dock, shown in Figure 1-6:

- **Safari** A web browser for surfing the Internet. With it you can create bookmarks, set a home page, and perform common tasks associated with the Internet.

- **Mail** A complete e-mail solution. With Mail, you can send and receive e-mail, save and manage e-mail, and perform common tasks associated with e-mailing.

- **Photos** An application for viewing and managing photos. With Photos, you can view slideshows, browse your photos, and even upload photos to the Web or import photos and videos from a digital camera or media card (provided you purchase the Apple Camera Connection Kit).

- **iPod** A complete music player that enables you to play and manage music. You can create playlists of your favorite songs or access playlists that have been synced from your home computer too, like Most Played.

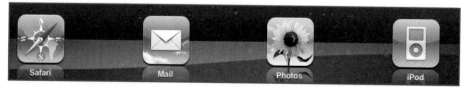

Figure 1-6: *There are four default icons that run across the bottom of all of the screens, but you can change these if you like and add additional icons, up to six.*

Learn Touch Techniques

You need to know the names of the components and iPad-related words to understand the description of the navigation techniques. Most importantly,

---

TIP

Tap any icon one time to open its associated app. Tap the **Home** button (the round button on the front of the iPad) to return to the Home screen.

the items on the Home screen are called *icons*, and you *tap* the icons to open their respective apps. When you open an app and tap in an area where you can type, the *virtual keyboard* appears. Tap the *keyboard icon* on the virtual keyboard to make the keyboard disappear. The keyboard is shown here.

QUICKSTEPS

USING TOUCH TECHNIQUES

There are plenty of ways to navigate your iPad with touch techniques or to use touch techniques to personalize it. Try the following techniques.

FLICK TO A NEW HOME SCREEN

Lightly touch an area of the Home screen that is not covered with an app, and drag your finger to the right. Repeat and drag your finger left two times, and then back again.

REPOSITION HOME SCREEN ICONS

Tap and hold any icon on the Home screen, and when the icons start to jiggle, let go. Tap and hold any icon, and then drag it to a different area of the screen to reposition it. To move an icon off the current screen to another, drag it to the left or right side of the screen. When the new screen appears, let it go to move it there. Press the **Home** button to apply changes.

DRAG TO CREATE A FOLDER

Tap and hold any icon on any screen, and when the icons start to jiggle, drag one icon to the top of a similar icon and let it go. When the new folder appears, tap the X in the new window to rename the folder. Press **Done** and then tap outside the new folder to return to the previous screen. Press the **Home** button once to apply. (To change it back, repeat these steps and drag the icons out of the folder to the screen.)

PINCH TO ZOOM IN OR OUT

Tap the **Safari** icon. On any webpage, put your thumb and forefinger together, put them on the webpage, and then make an outward pinching motion to zoom in on the page. Now, position your thumb and forefinger far apart, put them both on the page, and pull them together in an inward pinching motion to zoom back in.

In addition, there are various techniques beyond simply tapping:

- A *double-tap* is often used to zoom in on something like a photo or webpage.
- A *double-press* on the Home button opens up a small window that offers access to your currently running apps.
- A *pinch* with your thumb and forefinger (either by pinching outward or inward) on a photo, webpage, or other compatible media is used to zoom in and out.
- A *tap-and-hold* action on an icon causes the icons to "jiggle." You can then rearrange them on the screen by keeping your finger on an icon and *dragging* it to a new area or screen. You can also tap the X that appears on any jiggling third-party app to delete it. You tap the Home button to stop the icons from "jiggling."
- A *flick,* sometimes called a *swipe,* is used to move from the Home screen to any other screen you've created (and back). A flick is a quick motion in which you move your finger quickly from one side of the screen to another, or from top to bottom. Flick right from your default Home screen to access the Spotlight Search screen; flick left to return. Flick up or down to move quickly through data that is longer than one page, such as the contacts in your Contacts app or information on a webpage. You can also flick left and right to move to a new page in an e-book.

- After tapping and holding to make your icons "jiggle," *dragging* one icon on top of another enables you to create a new *folder.* Move similar apps into folders to organize them. Don't worry; you'll get to practice this shortly!

• Tapping works within apps in various ways, too. Tap twice in a video to view it in full-screen mode, and tap twice again to return to regular viewing; tap once on text to access menus such as Select, Select All, Copy, and Paste; and tap once in an app like iBooks to show or hide controls.

Personalize Your iPad

You can personalize your iPad in ways other than repositioning icons or creating folders. You can change the wallpaper, change under what circumstances sounds are played, and create a passcode that must be input before you can use your iPad. The latter can protect your iPad from unauthorized use. Along those same lines, you can also protect your iPad with a feature currently called *Find My iPad*, which enables you to locate your iPad via global positioning system (GPS) if it's ever lost or stolen.

Change the Wallpaper on Your iPad

You can apply wallpaper to the Home screen or the Lock screen, or both. The wallpaper you apply to the Home screen will be applied to any additional screens you create. *Wallpaper* is what you see behind the icons when using your iPad. The wallpaper you configure for your Lock screen is the picture you'll see when you wake your iPad but before you move the slider to use or unlock it. Wallpapers are shown in Figure 1-7, and are available from the Settings icon under Brightness & Wallpaper.

To change the wallpaper for the Home screen, the Lock screen, or both:

1. Tap **Settings**.

2. Tap **Brightness & Wallpaper**.

3. Tap the right-facing arrow in the Wallpaper section.

4. Tap the arrow by Wallpaper.

Brightness & Wallpaper

Auto-Brightness **ON**

Wallpaper

>

Settings window   Back button   Available wallpaper

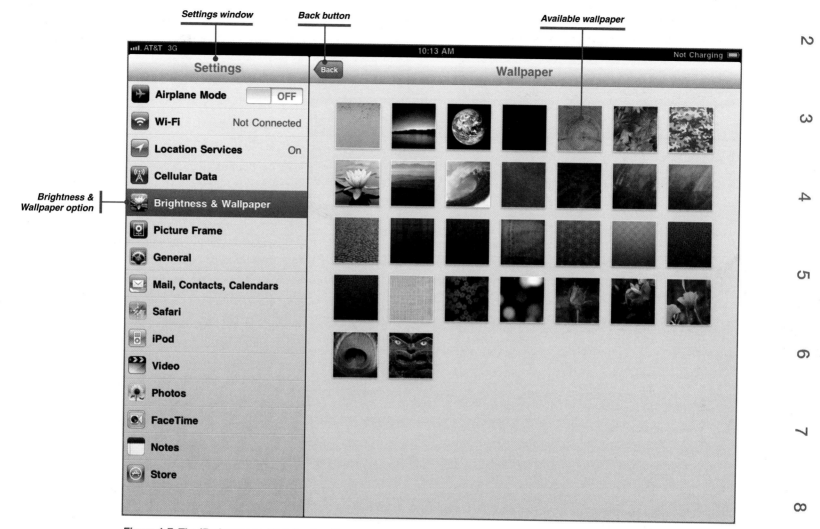

Brightness &
Wallpaper option

Figure 1-7: *The iPad comes with lots of wallpaper you can select from.*

5. Tap a wallpaper to apply it to either the Home screen or the Lock screen.

6. Tap **Set Lock Screen, Set Home Screen**, or **Set Both**.

7. Press the **Home button** to close the Settings app.

NOTE

Settings will open to the exact place you were the last time you used the Settings app. You can either tap whatever "back" button is available to return to a previous set of settings or simply tap an item in the left pane.

Configure Sounds

Sounds play when you get new mail, send mail, get a Calendar alert, lock the iPad, or tap a key on the keyboard. Sounds also play at a level you've set using the Volume buttons on the outside of the iPad. You can opt not to play any or all of these sounds inside the Settings app (and change the volume there too).

1. Tap **Settings**.

2. Tap **General**.

3. Tap **Sounds**.

4. To change the Ringtone setting, tap **Marimba** and tap a new sound.

5. To turn on and off sounds for specific events, tap the **On** (or **Off**) button for any sound option to change it. You can also preview any sound by turning the sound for the event off and then back on. To understand what each of these options means, refer to the bulleted list, next.

6. Move the slider to change the volume.

The various sound options are:

	10:17 AM	Not Charging
General	**Sounds**	

Ringer and Alerts

◀ ━━━━━━━━━●━━━━━━━━ ◀))

Change with Buttons   `OFF`

The volume of the ringer and alerts will not be affected by the volume buttons.

Ringtone   Marimba ›

New Mail   `ON`

Sent Mail   `ON`

Calendar Alerts   `ON`

Lock Sounds   `ON`

Keyboard Clicks   `ON`

- **Ringtone**   The sound that plays when a FaceTime call arrives. Marimba, the default, is a light, ten-note song that repeats until you answer the call. You can hear it by tapping **Ringtone** which opens a page with more options, and then **Marimba.**

- **New Mail**   The sound that plays when a new e-mail arrives in the Mail app. The sound is a bright, short "ding" sound that plays one time.

- **Send Mail**   The sound that plays when e-mail has been successfully sent. The sound that accompanies it is a "whoosh" sound that plays one time.

- **Calendar Alerts**   The sound that plays when a calendar entry you've configured with specific criteria in conjunction with a reminder have been met. It sounds like a high-pitched siren and plays twice.

TIP

You don't have to "save" changes you make in the Settings app or tap any "back" button to apply them. Changes are applied immediately with no further input required from you.

CAUTION

You won't increase security if you lock the iPad after a specific amount of idle time but do not apply a passcode lock. Without a passcode lock, you only need to move the slider to unlock the iPad.

TIP

You can also opt to lock the iPad after a specific amount of time to increase battery life.

2 Minutes	
5 Minutes	✓
10 Minutes	
15 Minutes	
Never	

Turn Passcode Off	
Change Passcode	
Require Passcode	Immediately >
Simple Passcode	ON

A simple passcode is a 4 digit number.

Picture Frame	ON
Erase Data	OFF

Erase all data on this iPad after 10 failed passcode attempts. Data protection is enabled.

- **Lock Sounds** The sound that plays when you lock your iPad. It sounds like a camera when taking a picture. It plays one time.
- **Keyboard Click** The sound that occurs when you tap a key on the keyboard. It's a short, low, staccato sound. A sound plays each time you tap a key.

Use Auto-Lock and Passcode Lock

It's important to protect your iPad from unauthorized use. Without precautions in place, anyone could pick up your iPad and use it. This means they could send e-mail as you, listen to your media and watch your videos, and more. You can protect your iPad by configuring it to lock automatically after a specific amount of idle time and by applying a four-digit passcode lock that must be entered before the iPad can be used again.

To enable Auto-Lock and Passcode Lock:

1. Tap **Settings** and tap **General**. The General window opens, shown in Figure 1-8.
2. Tap **Auto-Lock**.
3. Tap the desired number of minutes.
4. Click **General** to return to the previous screen.
5. Tap **Passcode Lock** and then tap **Turn Passcode On**.
6. Type a four-digit passcode, and then repeat the code.
7. Tap the arrow next to **Require Passcode**.
8. Choose how much time should pass before a passcode is required.
9. Tap **Passcode Lock** to return to the previous screen.

While configuring Passcode Lock, look at the other options, specifically Simple Passcode. If you turn off the Simple Passcode option, you can enter longer, more complex passcodes. It does not have to be a four-digit number. Note also the Erase Data option. If you enable this option, all of the data on the iPad will be erased after 10 failed passcode attempts.

Enable Find My iPad

If you lose your iPad, Find My iPad is available to help you locate it (provided the iPad is powered on). However, you have to set up the

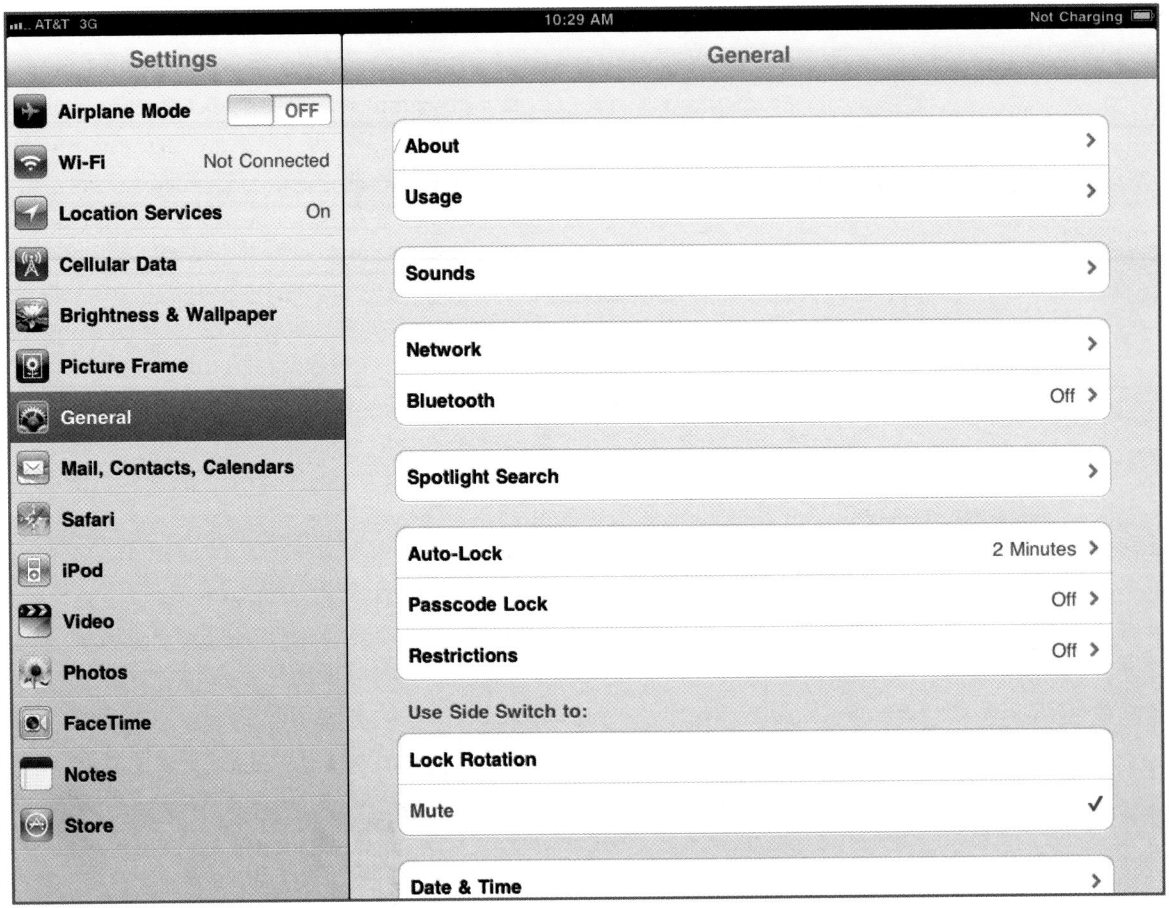

.ıl. AT&T 3G	10:29 AM	Not Charging ▬

Settings	General

Airplane Mode [OFF]

Wi-Fi   Not Connected

Location Services   On

Cellular Data

Brightness & Wallpaper

Picture Frame

General

Mail, Contacts, Calendars

Safari

iPod

Video

Photos

FaceTime

Notes

Store

About   ›

Usage   ›

Sounds   ›

Network   ›

Bluetooth   Off ›

Spotlight Search   ›

Auto-Lock   2 Minutes ›

Passcode Lock   Off ›

Restrictions   Off ›

Use Side Switch to:

Lock Rotation

Mute   ✓

Date & Time   ›

*Figure 1-8: **The General window offers access to Auto-Lock, Passcode Lock, and more.***

feature beforehand. This requires that you add the free MobileMe e-mail account and then confirm that account with Apple, which takes a bit of time, perhaps 5 or 10 minutes, but is certainly well worth it.

With Find My iPad you'll be able to sign in to www.Me.com anytime you've misplaced your iPad and see where it is on a map. Perhaps that's your living room, a coffee house, or a doctor's office; it doesn't matter. You can access www.Me.com from any Internet-enabled computer, phone, or tablet, so you can use almost any available device if your iPad is lost. Once you've located your iPad, you can send a message to be displayed on it that says "Oops, I left my iPad here. I'm on my way now to retrieve it"; or, if it's lost in your home or car, you can send a signal to your iPad to play a sound (and to override any volume setting you currently have configured) so that you can find it. Finally, you can remotely set a passcode lock to protect your iPad from prying eyes if you left it in a public place; or, if you've decided your iPad has been stolen and won't be returned, you can remotely wipe the data on it, erasing all sensitive and personal data at once (or at least the next time it's turned on).

Configuring Find My iPad involves several steps, all outlined very well at www.apple.com/ipad/find-my-ipad-setup. Because the steps may change as the feature evolves, you should visit this webpage when you're ready to configure it. In a nutshell:

Cancel	MobileMe	Next
Apple ID	joli_ballew@tx.rr.com	
Password	••••••••	

Use MobileMe with your Apple ID or MobileMe email address.

Create Free Apple ID   >

1. Tap **Settings** and tap **Mail, Contacts, Calendars**.
2. Tap the **Add Account** button, and tap **MobileMe**.
3. Enter your Apple ID and password.
4. Tap **Next**.
5. If prompted at any time during the process to let MobileMe use the location of your iPad, tap **OK**.
6. If this is the first time you've ever set up MobileMe or Find My iPad, you'll have to wait for a verification e-mail. Because you've likely yet to set up the Mail app, do this from your desktop or laptop computer.
7. After you've verified your e-mail, return to the MobileMe screen (which is still open and available on your iPad), and tap **Find My iPad** to turn it on.
8. Tap **Save**.
9. Wait for the verification e-mail to arrive in your inbox, and click the link offered. Input the required information.

*Figure 1-9: **Once you've found your iPad, you have options for retrieving or securing it.***

Once you've configured Find My iPad, it's easy to test it. Visit www.me.com, input your Apple ID and password, and click **Find My iPad**. Once logged in, you'll have access to the options shown in Figure 1-9. One of the options is to play a sound, which is useful if you've lost your iPad under a couch or left it in your car. You can also write a message to be displayed on your iPad if you think you've left it at a friend's house, for example. You can lock your iPad too, and if you think the iPad's been stolen and won't be returned, you can erase all of the data on it. (Find My iPad won't work if your iPad is not powered on.)

Choose a Data Plan

If you own a 3G-equipped iPad model, there are two ways to access the Internet. You can access the Internet through a Wi-Fi network like what you'll find at coffee shops, libraries, and possibly even your own home or workplace; or you can access the Internet using a data provider's cellular network, such as Verizon or AT&T. Wi-Fi is almost always free (although you may have to purchase a cup of coffee or get a library card), while 3G is something you have to pay for. Most of the time you'll want to find a Wi-Fi hotspot to connect because Wi-Fi is faster than 3G and the data you use won't be counted against any cellular data plan you may have signed up for.

When Wi-Fi isn't available, you'll need 3G access to connect to the Internet when you're out of range of a Wi-Fi hotspot. This involves choosing and paying for a 3G data plan from a data provider, because 3G service isn't free. You can only use 3G if you have a Wi-Fi + 3G iPad. If your iPad is Wi-Fi only, you're out of luck.

If you aren't sure if you have a Wi-Fi + 3G model or if you want to sign up for 3G service, tap **Settings** and tap **Cellular Data**. If you don't see the Cellular Data option, you don't have the 3G model. Tap **Cellular Data** to turn on the feature, configure data roaming, or view usage on your account. Figure 1-10 shows these options. If you have a 3G model but have not signed up for 3G,

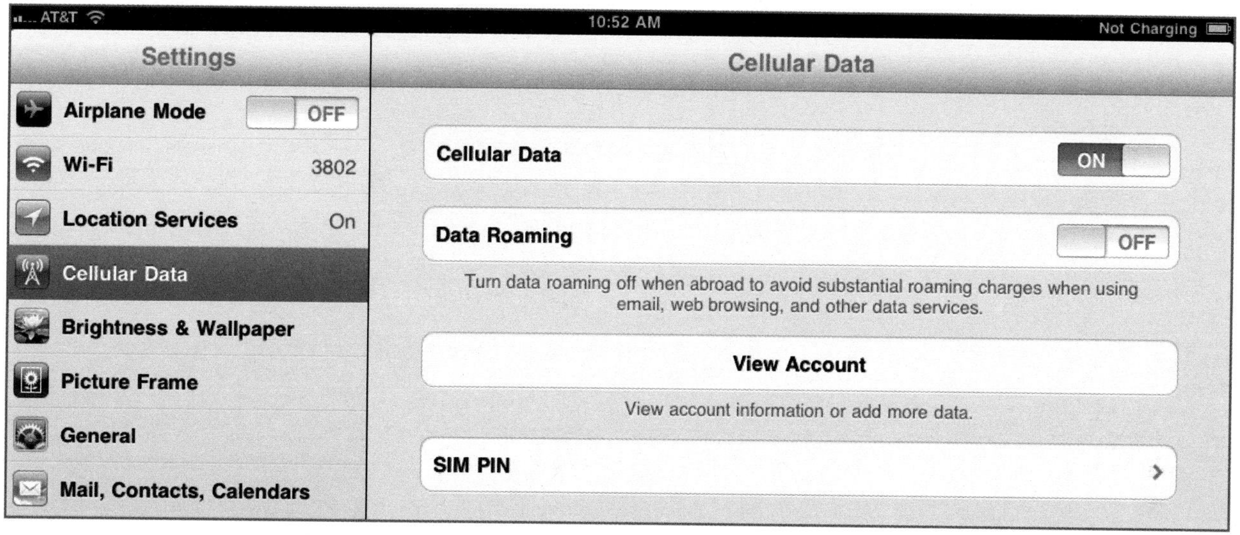

Figure 1-10: **The Settings app offers cellular data options on compatible iPad models.**

you won't see what's shown here; instead, you'll have the option to sign up for cellular data service.

You can see in Figure 1-10 that I've already signed up for data service and that Cellular Data is enabled. Notice that AT&T is shown in the top-left corner of the interface, reflecting my choice in data providers.

How to...

Chapter 2

Accessing and Surfing the Internet

The Internet provides easy access to worldwide information and news; local directions and maps; social networking applications and sites; and music, video, and games, among other things. For many, having easy access to the Internet is the main reason for purchasing an iPad.

This chapter explains how to access and use the Internet from your iPad and get the most from it. You'll learn the difference between Wi-Fi and cellular data and how to connect to the Internet with either; how to use Safari, a web browser included on your iPad, to surf the Internet once connected; and how to save bookmarks and configure Safari to keep you safe while you're online.

2

1
3
4
5
6
7
8
9
10

QUICK**FACTS**

UNDERSTANDING WI-FI AND CELLULAR DATA

There are two different networking models for the iPad. The first is Wi-Fi only, and the second is Wi-Fi + 3G.

WI-FI ONLY

The iPad Wi-Fi model connects to the Internet only one way: when you are within range of and have permission to use a Wi-Fi network. You may have a Wi-Fi network in your home or at work, and you can locate free Wi-Fi networks, called *hotspots*, in coffee shops, hotels, libraries, and similar establishments. You must be within range of a Wi-Fi network to get Internet access. There is no other way to get online.

WI-FI + 3G

The iPad Wi-Fi + 3G model connects to the Internet in two ways. One is through a Wi-Fi connection, described in the previous paragraph. The other is through a 3G connection available via cellular networks, typically offered by companies like AT&T or Verizon. If you have a Wi-Fi + 3G model, you can get online at free Wi-Fi hotspots, your wireless network at work and at home, and, when those aren't available, using a cellular network. Note that you have to pay for a 3G data plan to obtain cellular access.

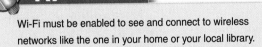

TIP

Wi-Fi must be enabled to see and connect to wireless networks like the one in your home or your local library.

Connect to the Internet

Every iPad is capable of connecting to the Internet over a Wi-Fi network. If you have a Wi-Fi + 3G model iPad, you can connect to the Internet in two ways. You can connect to the Internet through an Internet-enabled Wi-Fi network, or you can connect via a cellular data plan you pay for each month. Free public Wi-Fi networks are available in coffee shops, libraries, hotels, and the like, and personal Wi-Fi networks are available in homes and businesses and are often protected with a password. When a Wi-Fi network isn't available, and if you have a compatible iPad and data plan, you can connect to the Internet using a cellular data plan. You learned a little about all of this at the end of Chapter 1. Figure 2-1 shows the iPad connected to a Wi-Fi network and Safari open to the *New York Times* home page.

Connect to a Wi-Fi Network

To connect to a Wi-Fi network, your iPad's Wi-Fi feature must be enabled. When Wi-Fi is enabled, the iPad will constantly search for networks to connect to and will prompt you when one is within range.

To connect to an available network:

1. If a Wi-Fi network is available, and if your iPad is configured to prompt you when it finds available wireless networks, when prompted to join a network:

   a. Tap the prompt.

   b. Tap **Join**.

Figure 2-1: *Once connected to the Internet, you can surf the Web with Safari.*

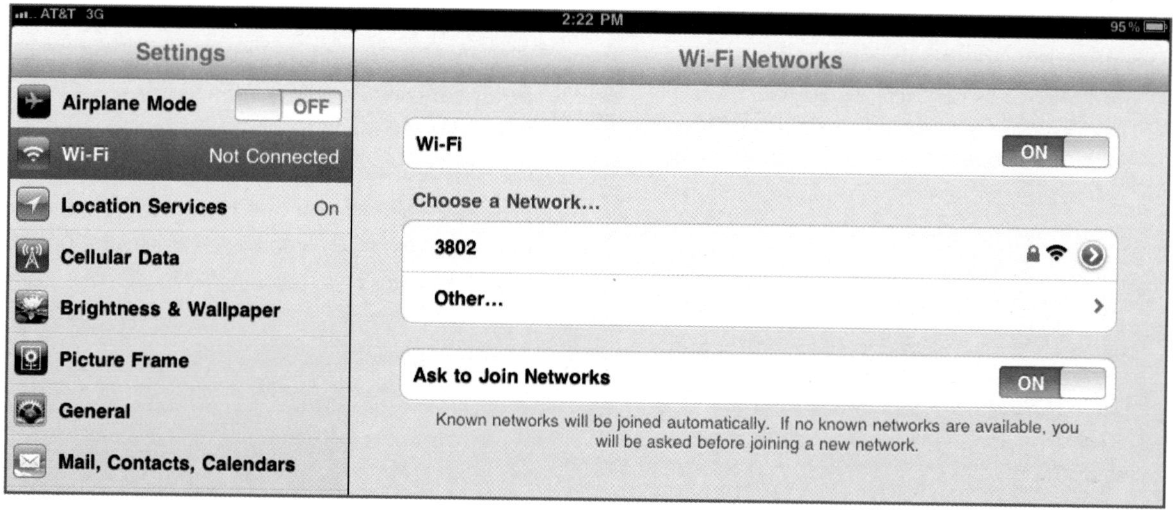

*Figure 2-2: **You can view available wireless networks.***

CAUTION

You will likely be charged extra from your cellular data provider when roaming. Thus, it's best to leave the Data Roaming feature turned off. If you're told you're out of range and you choose to roam, you can enable this feature then.

TIP

If you have a 3G data plan, leave Wi-Fi enabled at all times. This will ensure that you'll be connected to (or prompted to join) a Wi-Fi network when Wi-Fi is available. This will help limit your 3G data usage.

NOTE

Wi-Fi connections are almost always faster than 3G—another reason to opt for Wi-Fi when it's available.

2. To manually check for available wireless networks:
   a. Tap the **Settings** icon, and tap **Wi-Fi**.
   b. Under Choose A Network, tap any network to join it, as shown in Figure 2-2.
3. If prompted, enter the password and tap **Join**.
4. Tap the **Home** button to return to the Home screen.

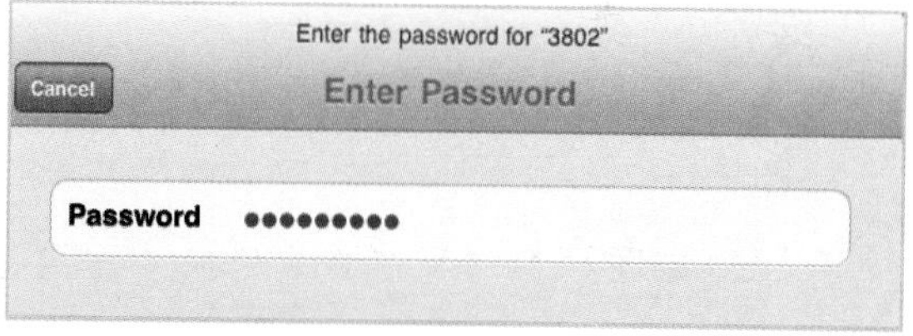

Monitor Cellular Data Usage

If you have a Wi-Fi + 3G iPad and pay for a data plan from a provider like AT&T, you can access the Internet from anywhere, at any time, provided you're within the service range. If you choose the plan that only allows a small amount of data usage per month, you'll want to watch just how often you use the 3G service; but if you have a more generous plan, there's less (or no) need to worry about usage.

QUICKSTEPS

ENABLING NETWORK CONNECTIONS

Your iPad's Wi-Fi feature must be enabled to connect to wireless networks. Likewise, your iPad's Wi-Fi + 3G Cellular Data feature must be enabled to connect using your cellular data plan. If you're having problems viewing and joining networks, make sure that the features you need are indeed enabled.

ENABLE WI-FI

1. From the Home screen, tap **Settings**.

2. In the left pane, tap **Wi-Fi**.

3. Move the **Wi-Fi** slider to **On**.

4. To be notified when Wi-Fi networks are available, move the **Ask To Join Networks** slider to **On**.

5. Tap the **Home** button to return to the Home screen.

ENABLE CELLULAR DATA

1. From the Home screen, tap **Settings**.

2. From the left pane, tap **Cellular Data**.

3. Move the **Cellular Data** slider to **On**.

4. To enable data roaming, move the **Data Roaming** slider to **On**.

5. Tap the **Home** button to return to the Home screen.

TIP

You can turn off any app's ability to obtain updates automatically or obtain information automatically from Settings. This enables you to control how an individual app accesses or retrieves information from the Internet. See Chapter 10 for more information about Settings options.

You will want to disable the Cellular Data feature anytime you are away from a Wi-Fi network and don't want Mail and other apps to retrieve data or check for updates when you don't need them to. Some apps receive data from the Internet routinely, like social networking apps that get status updates behind the scenes or news apps that you configure or allow to offer pop-ups about breaking news. If you don't need to view these updates and are keeping an eye on your data usage, you can disable the Cellular Data feature when you aren't using the iPad.

To see how much data you've used during your current cellular data billing cycle or to change your data plan:

1. Tap **Settings**.

2. Tap **Cellular Data**.

3. Tap **View Account**. See Figure 2-3.

4. Tap next to **email**. Type the e-mail address you used to activate your iPad.

5. Tap next to **password**. Type the password.

6. Tap **Go**.

7. Review the information provided.

8. Tap **Add Data Or Change Plan**, **Add International Plan**, or **Edit User & Payment Information** to make changes, if desired, and work through any additional pages.

9. Tap **OK** when finished.

Wi-Fi Networks

Wi-Fi	ON
Choose a Network...	
✓ 3802	
Other...	>
Ask to Join Networks	ON

Known networks will be joined automatically. If no known networks are available, you will be asked before joining a new network.

Cellular Data Account   Cancel

Rethink Possible

Account Overview
Cellular Data Number: 214-842-7697

data plan	250 MB of domestic data per month
status	105 MB used / 145 MB left for 12 days
billing period	03/17/11 to 04/16/11

Add Data or Change Plan	>
Add International Plan	>
Edit User & Payment Information	>

View Full Account Overview...

OK

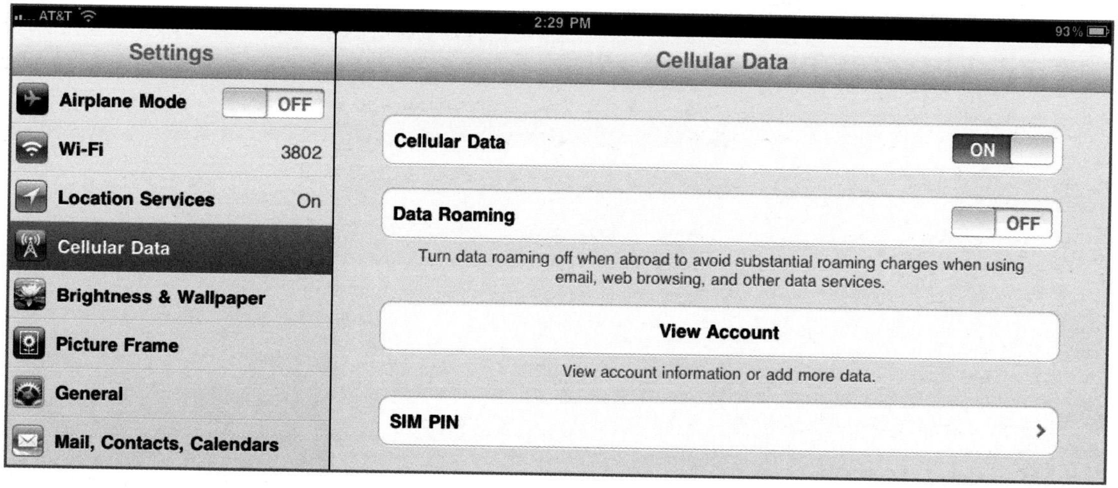

Figure 2-3: You can keep track of your data usage by viewing your account information.

Use Safari

Safari is the web browser that comes preinstalled on your iPad, and you use it to surf the Internet. It's a full browser; with it you can locate anything on the Web, view just about any webpage, view lots of types of web media, save and manage bookmarks for websites you visit often, and more. There are two views, Landscape and Portrait; you can zoom in and out of a page easily; and you can have multiple webpages open at once and switch among them with just a couple of taps with your finger.

As with other web browsers you've used, Safari offers easy-to-recognize icons, keeps track of the websites you've visited in the past, and when you type in a web address, offers addresses that start with the letters you've typed. If you see what you want in the resulting list, you can tap the suggestion to go there. You can also add icons for webpages you visit often right on the Home screen or the Bookmarks Bar, which you'll learn about later in this chapter. Safari is shown in Figure 2-4.

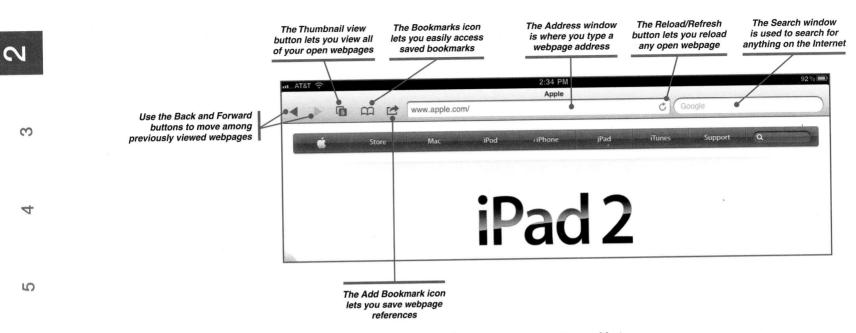

The Thumbnail view button lets you view all of your open webpages

The Bookmarks icon lets you easily access saved bookmarks

The Address window is where you type a webpage address

The Reload/Refresh button lets you reload any open webpage

The Search window is used to search for anything on the Internet

Use the Back and Forward buttons to move among previously viewed webpages

The Add Bookmark icon lets you save webpage references

Figure 2-4: **Safari is a complete web browser and offers plenty of features.**

TIP

Safari is available from the Home screen by default, and is one of the four icons displayed across the bottom of the screen, on the Dock.

NOTE

Before you can use Safari to surf the Web, you have to be connected to a network that offers Internet access.

Visit a Webpage

There are several ways you can visit a webpage:

- Type the address of the webpage in the Address window. This is called a Uniform Resource Locator (URL).

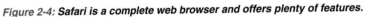

- Tap a link in a webpage. Link is short for *hyperlink* and offers one-tap access to another webpage.

Joli Ballew
Writer

work   **(972) 555-5555**

work   **Joli_Ballew@hotmail.com**

home   **joli_ballew@hotmail.com**

other   **joli_ballew@tx.rr.com**

home page   **www.JoliBallew.com**

home   **Joli_Ballew@hotmail.com (AIM)**

- Tap any bookmark on the Bookmarks Bar or in the Bookmarks list. A bookmark offers one-tap access to a page you visit often. (You'll learn more about bookmarks later in this chapter.)

- Tap the **Back** or **Forward** buttons when applicable. The Back and Forward buttons are only active after you've visited a few webpages.

- Tap a URL in a contact card, e-mail, document, or other medium. URLs are often called webpages.

To navigate to a webpage using the Address window:

1. Tap **Safari** on the Home screen.

2. Tap the Address window.

3. Tap the **X** in the Address window to clear any existing URLs.

> Apple - iPad - All-new design. Video calls. HD video. And more.
>
> http://www.apple.com/ipad/   ⊗

4. Type <u>mcgrawhill</u> and tap the **.com** key.

5. Tap **Go**.

TIP

Safari will automatically insert the "http://" and the "www." if you don't type it.

NOTE

All websites offer links to other webpages. Click any link to navigate to a different webpage.

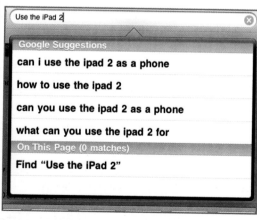

> Use the iPad 2| ⊗
>
> **Google Suggestions**
>
> **can i use the ipad 2 as a phone**
>
> **how to use the ipad 2**
>
> **can you use the ipad 2 as a phone**
>
> **what can you use the ipad 2 for**
>
> On This Page (0 matches)
>
> **Find "Use the iPad 2"**

Figure 2-5: The Search window offers suggestions as you type.

Perform a Search

The Search window in Safari offers an easy way to search for anything on the Internet. To perform a search, you simply tap inside the window, and when the virtual keyboard appears, type your keywords. If what you're looking for appears underneath, tap it to see the results. If not, click **Search** on the keyboard. Figure 2-5 shows an example.

TIP

Visit www.cnn.com and click any video to view it. CNN is iPad-compatible and does not require you to have Adobe Flash to play their videos.

View Media

Media you find on the Web will generally consist of pictures, videos, and music. Most of the time, you only need tap the media to view it or hear it. You can't view all of the media on the Web, however, because you can't view media that uses Adobe Flash. That's a limitation, but many websites are now offering their videos without this requirement.

Some apps are designed specifically for viewing specific types of media, too. For instance, if you have a Netflix subscription, you can view the "Watch Instantly" movies that Netflix offers using its free Netflix app. If you missed your favorite television show on ABC, the ABC Player app lets you watch it on your iPad. HBO, Showtime, and others have similar apps. There are even apps that will "show you," with video, how to cook a recipe or perform first aid, among other things.

UICKSTEPS

LOCATING AND VIEWING MEDIA

1. Tap **Safari** and navigate to www.apple.com.

2. If applicable, click the **iPad** tab at the top of the page.

3. In the iPad webpage, click **Guided Tours**.

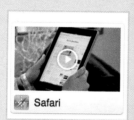

4. Scroll down and tap **Safari**.

5. While the video plays, tap to access the video controls.

6. To stop the video, tap it. Controls will appear that you can use to pause the video and then start playing it again. You can also opt to view the video in full-screen mode.

7. Tap the **Back** button, and tap **Guided Tours** again to locate the Guided Tours page. Later, you'll create a bookmark for it so you can view other videos as time allows.

UICKSTEPS

ZOOMING, SCROLLING, AND GETTING BACK TO THE TOP OF THE PAGE

Practice these touch techniques in Safari to see how they are applied in this medium.

PINCH TO ZOOM

On any webpage (or use the Guided Tours webpage if you're still on that page from the last exercise), put your thumb and forefinger together and pull them outward

Continued . . .

Incorporate Touch Techniques

You interact with Safari using one or two fingers. You can tap, pinch, and flick to access media, zoom in and out, and scroll, among other things. You may remember these terms from Chapter 1. In addition, you can easily switch from Portrait to Landscape mode by rotating your iPad 90 degrees left or right, and you can flip the iPad to turn the page upside-down, perhaps to show the page to a person sitting across from you.

The most common navigational touch techniques are:

- **Tap** to use the Back and Forward buttons, navigate to new webpages through links, go to any page you've bookmarked (which you may not have done yet), bring up the keyboard in any window that allows you to type in it, and more.

0:27 -1:26

- **Pinch** to zoom in or out on any webpage, picture, or video.
- **Flick** to scroll through a page that runs longer than the length of the screen.
- **Rotate** or **Flip** rotate the iPad 90 degrees to switch from Portrait to Landscape mode or Landscape to Portrait mode, or flip it completely over to show the page to a person sitting across from you.

Use Bookmarks

A bookmark is a shortcut to a webpage you visit often or would like to find easily later. There are a few bookmarks already in place, including Apple, Google, and Yahoo!, and a link to the iPad User Guide. These particular bookmarks appear in the Bookmarks list, available with a single tap after you tap the Bookmarks icon (see Figure 2-6). There are two other options as well, *History*, which offers a list of websites you've recently visited, and *Bookmarks Bar*, which contains bookmarks you save and want displayed at the top of your browser window for easy access.

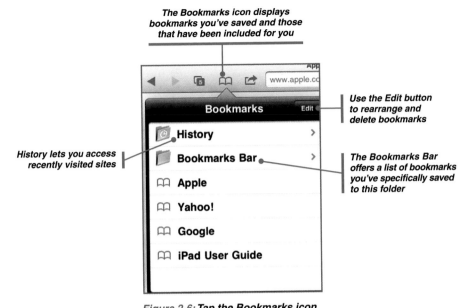

The Bookmarks icon displays bookmarks you've saved and those that have been included for you

Use the Edit button to rearrange and delete bookmarks

History lets you access recently visited sites

The Bookmarks Bar offers a list of bookmarks you've specifically saved to this folder

Figure 2-6: *Tap the Bookmarks icon to access the Bookmarks list, History, and the items in the Bookmarks Bar.*

ZOOMING, SCROLLING, AND GETTING BACK TO THE TOP OF THE PAGE (Continued)

to zoom in on the webpage. You can zoom in or out on a picture or text, too. If a video is playing, you can use the pinching motion to switch from the current, smaller webpage view to full-screen view. Use a reverse pinching motion to zoom back out of any text, picture, webpage, or video.

FLICK TO SCROLL

On any webpage that is longer than the length of the screen, flick from the bottom of the page up to scroll down the page. Flick from the top of the page down to scroll up the page.

TAP TO GET TO THE TOP OF A PAGE QUICKLY

If you've scrolled down the page, tap at the top of the screen (perhaps above the Address window) to return to the top of a webpage quickly.

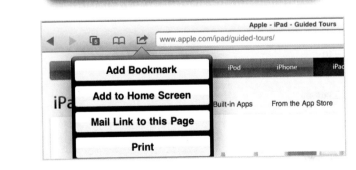

TIP

If you're an avid Internet Explorer user, a bookmark is the same as a favorite.

To make sites you visit regularly easier to access, you can add a bookmark for them in the Bookmarks list. If you're still on the Guided Tours page of the Apple website, add a bookmark for it. To add a bookmark to the Bookmark list:

1. Tap **Safari** and navigate to the page for which you'd like to add a bookmark.

2. Tap the **Add Bookmark** icon, and tap **Add Bookmark**.

3. If desired, use the keyboard to type a new name.

4. Verify that **Bookmarks** is selected. If Bookmarks Bar is displayed instead, tap **Bookmarks Bar** and then tap **Bookmarks**.

5. Tap **Save**.

TIP

Create a web clip on your Home screen for websites you access often, such as social networking sites, a blog you write, or web-based e-mail.

TIP

You can view the Bookmarks Bar by tapping the Address window. To show the Bookmarks Bar permanently, from the Home screen, tap **Settings**, tap **Safari**, and move the **Always Show Bookmarks Bar** slider to **On**, as detailed later.

TIP

Consider creating a Bookmark folder named Travel, and put links to all of your favorite travel-related websites there. Create additional folders named Help Pages, Apple, Job Hunting, Real Estate, or any other thing to organize other bookmarks you want to keep.

If there's a website you visit often, you can put an icon for that webpage on your Home screen. This is called a *web clip*. It gives you one-tap access to the page.

To save a webpage as a web clip:

1. Tap **Safari** and navigate to your favorite webpage.
2. Tap the **Add Bookmark** icon.
3. Tap **Add To Home Screen**.
4. If desired, change the name offered, and then tap **Add**.
5. Note the new icon on the Home screen.

To add a bookmark to the Bookmarks Bar and then view that bookmark:

1. Tap **Safari** and navigate to a favorite webpage.
2. Tap the **Add Bookmark** icon.
3. Tap **Add Bookmark**.
4. If desired, change the name offered.
5. Tap **Bookmarks**.
6. Tap **Bookmarks Bar**.
7. Tap **Save**.
8. To view the new bookmark, tap inside the Address window to show the Bookmarks Bar.

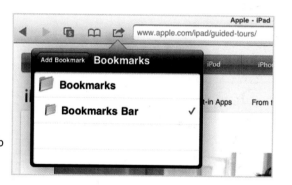

QUICKSTEPS

CREATING AND MOVING BOOKMARK FOLDERS

Bookmark folders can be created in two places: the Bookmarks list and the Bookmarks Bar.

CREATE A BOOKMARK FOLDER IN THE BOOKMARKS LIST

To create a new bookmark folder on the Bookmarks list:

1. Tap the **Bookmark** icon on the toolbar.

2. Tap **Edit**.

3. Tap **New Folder**.

4. Type a name for the folder.

5. Verify that **Bookmarks** is displayed. (If Bookmarks Bar is displayed instead, tap it and then tap **Bookmarks**.)

6. Tap **Bookmarks**.

7. Tap **Done**.

CREATE A BOOKMARK FOLDER IN THE BOOKMARKS BAR

To create a new bookmark folder on the Bookmarks Bar:

1. Tap the **Bookmark** icon on the toolbar.

2. Tap **Edit**.

3. Tap **New Folder**.

4. Type a name for the folder.

5. Verify that **Bookmarks Bar** is displayed. (If Bookmarks is displayed instead, tap it and then tap **Bookmarks Bar**.)

Continued . . .

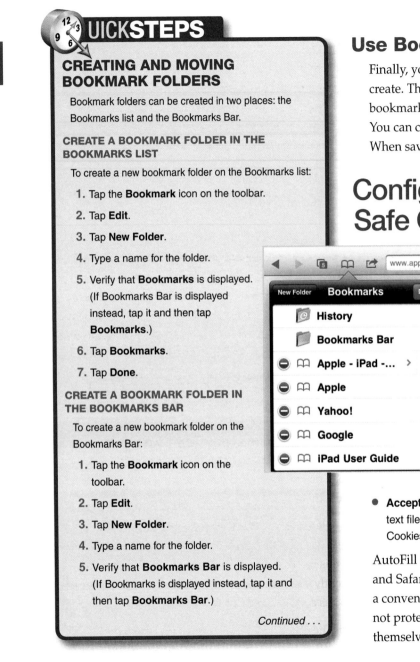

Use Bookmark Folders

Finally, you can organize the bookmarks you keep in bookmark folders you create. This is often a better solution than simply having a single, long list of bookmarks, a cluttered Bookmarks Bar, or a Home screen filled with web clips. You can create these folders on the Bookmarks Bar or in the Bookmarks list. When saving bookmarks, you can save them to these folders easily.

Configure Settings to Stay Safe Online

Safari helps you maintain your safety and privacy while on the Internet. Settings that Safari deems optimal are already set, but it's always a good idea to review them. You can also clear your History, Cookies, and Cache, among other things.

The following security settings are enabled by default:

- **Fraud Warning**   Enabled to warn you when you visit a fraudulent site that may try to get you to provide personal information or information about your bank account or credit cards. Some fraudulent websites also try to infect computers and devices with adware, spyware, and viruses.

- **Block Pop-ups**   Enabled to block pop-ups from websites that initiate them. Pop-ups are generally advertisements, and open in a new window.

- **Accept Cookies**   Enabled to accept cookies from websites you visit. Cookies are small text files that are stored on your iPad that tell a website what you prefer when visiting. Cookies can include your name, browsing history on the site, and items you've purchased.

AutoFill is not enabled by default. When you enable AutoFill, you tell your iPad and Safari that you want it to populate web forms automatically. While this is a convenience, it can also cause a security problem. If your iPad is stolen and is not protected by a passcode, the thief can access Safari and populate the forms themselves.

QUICKSTEPS

6. Tap **Bookmarks**.

7. Tap **Done**.

8. In the Bookmarks list, tap **Bookmarks Bar**.

9. Note the new folder.

MOVE A BOOKMARK INTO A FOLDER

To move a bookmark into a folder:

1. Tap the **Bookmark** icon.

2. Locate the folder that contains the bookmark you want to move. You may have to click the Back button, the Bookmarks Bar, a folder you created, or another item.

3. Tap **Edit**.

4. Tap a bookmark you created that you'd like to move.

5. In the Edit Bookmark window, tap **Bookmarks** or **Bookmarks Bar**, or whatever appears at the bottom of that window.

6. Tap the folder you want to move the bookmark to.

7. Tap **Bookmarks** to return to the Bookmarks list.

8. Tap **Done**.

NOTE

Chapter 10 introduces all of the available settings in Safari. This section only discusses what you need to stay safe while online.

Change Your Settings

You can change settings and preferences related to Safari for a better browsing experience from the Settings app on the Home screen. You can configure what search engine to use; whether or not to automatically fill in web forms with your name, address, and the like; and whether or not you want to show the Bookmarks Bar permanently in Safari. To access the settings:

1. Tap **Settings**.

2. Tap **Safari**.

3. Note the options in the right pane, shown in Figure 2-7.

One thing you may want to configure in the Safari settings options is to always show the Bookmarks Bar. When enabled, the bookmarks you've saved to the Bookmarks Bar will appear below the current options and just above the webpage. Figure 2-8 shows an example of a Bookmarks Bar. Here, iPad Guided Tours, iGoogle, Facebook, and Yahoo! are readily available. Move the slider for Always Show Bookmarks Bar from Off to On in Settings under Safari, if you'd like to try it.

Clear Cache, Cookies, and History

When you opt to let Safari accept cookies from sites you visit, you will have a better browsing experience. Websites can greet you by name and remember what you last shopped for and further personalize your visit to the site. You may want to clear cookies if you plan to loan or sell your iPad; you would not want others to be able to access this information.

Likewise, you may want to delete the list that Safari keeps of the websites you've recently visited. This is your history, and it can be viewed in Safari under the Bookmarks icon. While this is a convenience for you and enables you to return to webpages you recently visited but did not bookmark, it can give away information to anyone who has access to your iPad.

Finally, Safari keeps a cache. The cache contains some of the content of the websites you've recently visited so that Safari can pull this information from

Figure 2-7: *You can configure several items to personalize Safari.*

Figure 2-8: **The Bookmarks Bar offers easy access to your favorite bookmarks.**

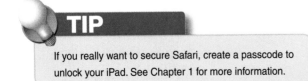

TIP

If you really want to secure Safari, create a passcode to unlock your iPad. See Chapter 1 for more information.

here instead of downloading it every time from the Internet. This helps control data usage and helps webpages you've previously visited load faster. If you notice you're not seeing the most up-to-date information, logos, status updates, or pictures on a page, which is unlikely, you should clear the cache.

To clear any of these things:

1. Tap **Settings**.

2. Tap **Safari**.

3. Tap **Clear History**, **Clear Cookies**, and/or **Clear Cache** as desired.

How to...

- Sync Your E-mail Accounts Using iTunes
- Add a MobileMe, Gmail, Yahoo!, or AOL Account
- Add Another Account Type
- Reading E-mail Messages on Multiple Devices
- Read E-mail
- Create a New E-mail
- Sending a Test E-mail
- Respond to E-mail
- E-mail Multiple Photos
- Use Gestures to Manage E-mail
- Open an Attachment
- Sending Videos
- Search for an E-mail
- Configuring Mail Settings
- Distinguishing Between Fetch and Push

Chapter 3

Communicating with Mail

The iPad comes with Mail, an e-mail management program already built in and ready to configure and use, available from the Home screen. With it you can easily view, receive, send, and reply to and forward e-mail; open many types of attachments; and even e-mail pictures of your own to others.

Before you can use Mail, you have to tell Mail about your e-mail accounts. This requires you to provide your e-mail addresses and password, and possibly, any associated settings, and that you test the e-mail accounts you configure to make sure they're working properly. Once you've done that, you're ready to use Mail.

Configure an E-mail Account

Your iPad comes with built-in support for e-mail accounts from Yahoo!, Gmail, AOL, and MobileMe, as well as Microsoft Exchange accounts, typically used in larger enterprises. This means that setup is extremely easy for these types of accounts, because Mail knows all of the required settings already and can configure them for you. You only need to know your user name and password to get started.

Mail also supports e-mail accounts from Internet service providers (ISPs) like Time Warner, Comcast, Verizon, and the like, although setting up these accounts sometimes takes a little more effort than the web-based e-mail services mentioned earlier. Whatever your situation, your first step in using Mail is to configure the accounts you want to use.

Sync Your E-mail Accounts Using iTunes

In this chapter, we outline how to set up your e-mail accounts manually, using your iPad. However, if you're going to use the same e-mail accounts on your iPad that you already have configured on *the computer you use to sync with it*, you can sync the mail account settings using iTunes, and you won't have to input them manually as detailed here.

It's important to note that only the settings will be synced unless you say so otherwise from the other tabs in iTunes. Syncing e-mail settings won't sync your contacts, calendar events, and the like; that's an additional option. There's also no way to sync the folders or e-mail messages that are already on your computer in your e-mail program. When you opt to sync in this manner, you're only syncing the settings and nothing else (not even your passwords).

To sync e-mail accounts using iTunes:

1. Connect your iPad to the computer you've been using to set up and sync your iPad. Make sure to connect to the computer you've been using since the beginning; do not connect your iPad to a different computer now, thinking that you'll just sync your mail accounts from it and nothing else; that won't work.

2. Wait while the initial syncing completes.

NOTE
You can't send or receive e-mail unless you are connected to the Internet.

TIP
If you're in the market for a new e-mail address, consider one from Google, Hotmail (aka Windows Live), AOL, or Yahoo! With it, you can easily configure your iPad and access mail from any computer you have access to that also has access to the Internet.

NOTE

If you have already created one e-mail account (or synced one using iTunes) and want to create another, tap **Settings** on the Home screen, and tap **Mail, Contacts, Calendars** to access the option to add a new account.

NOTE

You can get e-mail on your iPad and then retrieve the messages again at your home or office computer the next time you log on, even if you delete them in Mail.

3. At your computer, in iTunes, select your iPad.

4. Click the **Info** tab.

5. Select **Sync Mail Accounts From**, and select the e-mail program you use from the list (see Figure 3-1).

6. Click **Apply**.

7. When syncing completes, from your iPad, tap **Settings**.

8. Tap **Mail, Contacts, Calendars**.

9. Tap the mail account you just synced, and type your password. Tap **Done**.

Address	joliballew@gmail.com
Password	●●●●●●●●

Add a MobileMe, Gmail, Yahoo!, or AOL Account

To configure a web-based e-mail account like Yahoo! Mail, Gmail, AOL, or Mobile Me (MobileMe is a subscription service available from Apple):

1. On the Home screen, tap **Mail**.

2. Tap the option that matches the type of account you want to configure (see Figure 3-2). If your web-based e-mail account isn't listed (Windows Live, for example), refer to the next section to configure that account (you'll have to tap **Other**).

Summary Info Apps Music Movies TV Shows Podcasts iTunes U Books Photos

☑ **Sync Mail Accounts from** [Outlook ‡]

Selected Mail accounts

☑ Joli_Ballew@tx.rr.com (POP:Joli_ballew@tx.rr.com)
☑ joli@joliballew.com (POP:Joli@joliballew.com)
☐ Washington.mrs@gmail.com (IMAP:Washington.mrs@...

Syncing Mail accounts syncs your account settings, but not your passwords or messages. To enter passwords, add accounts, or make other changes, tap Settings then Mail, Contacts, Calendars on this iPad.

Figure 3-1: If you use the same e-mail accounts on your computer that you want to use on your iPad, you can sync the mail account settings from iTunes.

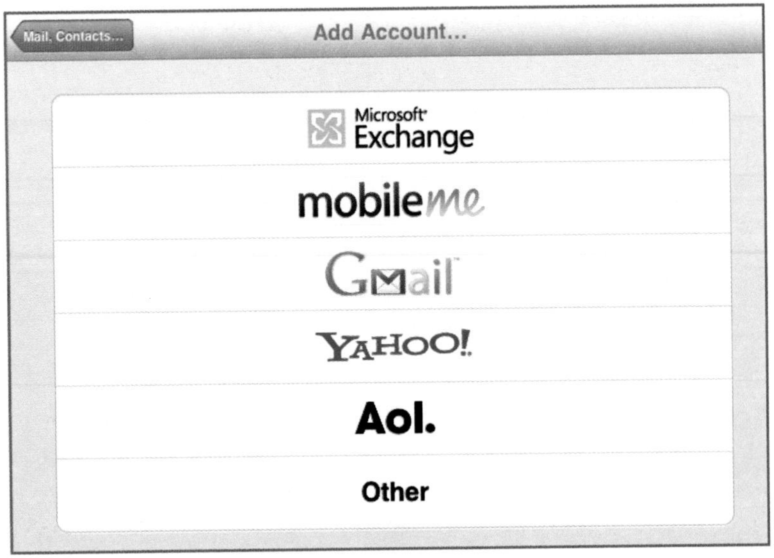

Figure 3-2: *Mail can configure various kinds of e-mail accounts automatically.*

3. Type the required information. You should only need to type your user name, e-mail address, password, and a description, shown in Figure 3-3.

4. Tap **Next**. Wait while the account settings are verified.

5. You may be prompted to configure additional settings, including whether or not to also download calendars, notes, and the like. Make choices as desired, and tap **Save**.

Add Another Account Type

If your e-mail account type isn't listed and you have to tap Other when setting up Mail, perhaps because you get your e-mail address from an Internet service you pay for, like Time Warner, Comcast, Verizon, or the like, you will probably have to provide some information manually. You'll be prompted for the information if it's required. If you don't know what to provide, call your Internet service provider for the details.

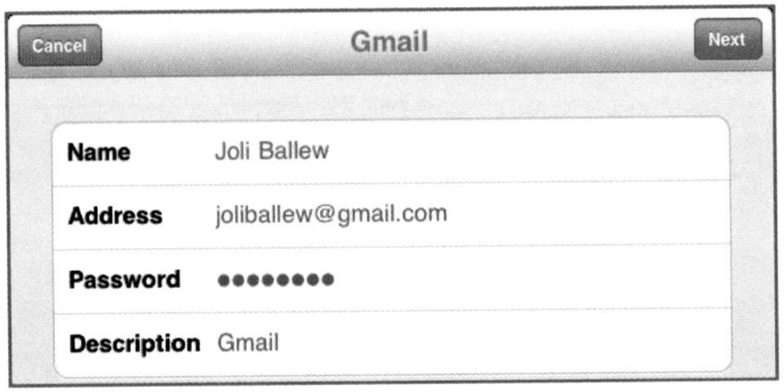

TIP

If you're having trouble inputting the required information, try these typing tips:

- If you need to capitalize a letter, touch the **Up** arrow.

- If you need to locate an underscore, dash, or similar character, touch the **.?123** key. Note you may have to touch the **#+=** key to access additional characters.

TIP

If you need to configure a Microsoft Exchange account, ask your network administrator at work to help you.

Figure 3-3: *When creating an account manually, you'll have to input your user name and password, among other things.*

NOTE

ISPs and e-mail providers store e-mail messages on large computer servers until you download the messages. Mail must know the server names and settings in order to download your e-mail from your e-mail provider, which is why you may have to provide this information in step 5 and perhaps troubleshoot it in step 6.

NOTE

If you see an error after manually providing information, tap **Settings** on the Home screen, tap **Mail, Contacts, Calendars**, tap the problematic account, and tap **Advanced**. Make changes as required.

TIP

If you get errors after setting up your e-mail account, call your ISP and ask them to help you with the settings. In some instances, you must enable or disable specific advanced settings.

NOTE

Mail is laid out such that Mailboxes is the starting place for Mail. While in the Mailboxes view, there is no button in the top-left corner of the page. When you leave that view to access another view, a new icon will appear. The icon that appears in the top-left corner while in landscape view is ultimately a "back" button.

To create an e-mail account in Mail for a POP3 e-mail account:

1. If you're already in Mail and creating an account, tap **Other**. Otherwise:

   a. On the Home screen, tap **Settings**.

   b. Tap **Mail, Contacts, Calendars**.

   c. Tap **Add Account**.

   d. Tap **Other**.

2. Tap **Add Mail Account**.

3. Type your e-mail name, e-mail address, password, and description of the account.

4. Tap **Save**.

5. If prompted, type any required information for the server names, host names, user names, and so on. You can get this information from your e-mail provider. Tap **Save**.

6. To edit the account, tap **Mail, Contacts, Calendars** and tap the account name. Figure 3-4 shows what you'll see, and you'll have the option to reenter information if you've encountered errors during the setup process.

Figure 3-4: You will have to edit the information if you encounter errors.

QUICKFACTS

READING E-MAIL MESSAGES ON MULTIPLE DEVICES

THE PROBLEM

Some e-mail providers that are categorized as *Other* have their own e-mail servers in which to store e-mail until you retrieve it. Unlike web-based servers (AOL, Gmail, Hotmail, etc.), these providers will often delete e-mail after you've downloaded it once, generally to your computer at work or at home. E-mail providers do this to manage the data stored on their e-mail servers so they don't fill up with unwanted data.

THE RESULT

If your e-mail provider deletes e-mail from their servers after you've downloaded it, and if you get your e-mail at one of these computers before you can retrieve it on your iPad, the e-mail won't be available for download. It will have already been removed (or downloaded) from the server.

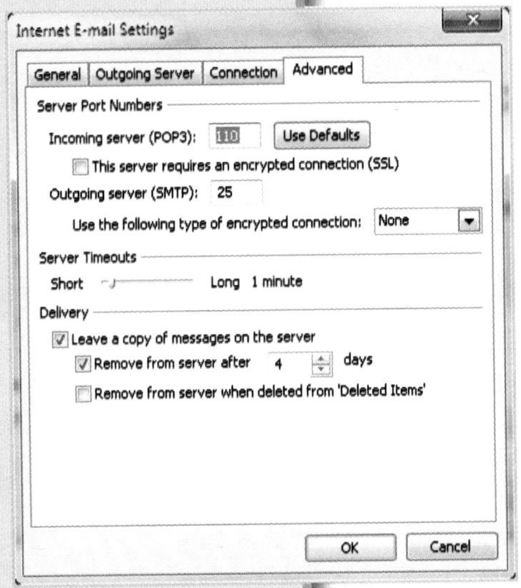

THE SOLUTION

Configure your home and/or work computer(s) to *leave a copy of the messages on the server* for a specified period. You'll need to open the e-mail program you use to get your mail and then search the Help files for something like "How to read email messages on multiple computers." Once you know how to make the change, do so on every computer you get e-mail on.

Work with E-mail

To read incoming mail and create your own, you first tap **Mail** to open it. If you've input more than one e-mail account, the first time you open Mail the *Mailboxes* page will appear and all of the accounts will be shown. (Subsequent visits to Mail will result in the app opening in the last view you used.) If this is the case, you can either tap a specific account to view only mail from that account, or you can tap **All Inboxes** to read all of your mail from all of your accounts in one window (see Figure 3-5).

Read E-mail

To read all of your e-mail from every configured account (assuming you have multiple e-mail accounts configured):

1. Tap **Mail** on the Home screen.
2. Rotate the iPad so you are in landscape view.
3. If the Mailboxes page appears, under Inboxes, tap **All Inboxes**.
4. Notice that a new button appears in the top-left part of the mail window: Mailboxes. You could tap **Mailboxes** to return to the previous screen (see Figure 3-6).
5. Tap any e-mail to read it, also shown in Figure 3-6.

Figure 3-5: If you've configured more than one e-mail account, you'll have access to all of them in Mailboxes view.

Figure 3-6: When in any inbox or folder, a new option may appear allowing you to return to previous screens.

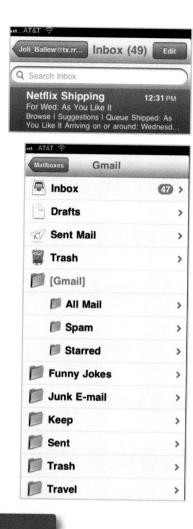

To read e-mail from only one specific account:

1. Tap **Mail**.

2. If required, tap **Mailboxes** to return to the Mailboxes view.

3. In Mailboxes, under Inboxes, tap any inbox listed.

4. To return to the previous screen, tap the account name.

In Mailboxes view there's also an *Accounts* section. Tap an account name here to gain access to any account's Inbox, Drafts, Sent, and Trash folders, as well as other folders, if they exist. From this view you can review your sent items, access drafts (these are e-mails you've started and saved but have not sent), and even review what's been deleted (in Trash). To return to previous tiers from inside these views, click the "back" button. The name of the button will change depending on where in the hierarchy you are.

When reading e-mail, you'll notice various arrows and buttons to help you navigate the interface, as well as options to enable you to perform tasks, such as delete an e-mail or reply to it. You'll see information across the top of the page to let you know you are connected to the Internet and options to access additional e-mail accounts. Figure 3-7 shows the icons that appear while reading an e-mail in landscape view.

TIP

Gmail and a few other web-based e-mail accounts will sync folders you've created at the website. This means you can create folders using your computer while, say, at the Gmail website, move data into them, and that information will be available from the Accounts section as shown in the illustration when you access it from your iPad.

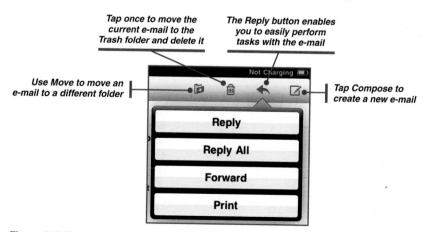

Figure 3-7: There are numerous icons in the Mail window when reading e-mail.

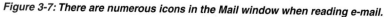

It's best to view Mail in landscape view for now. In landscape view you have easier access to all of the features. Portrait view does not offer the same amenities and can be more difficult to navigate.

Create a New E-mail

To start a new e-mail, tap the **Compose** button. The Compose button is available in all Mail windows, even Mailboxes and an account's Trash folder. After tapping Compose, a new e-mail will open, along with the virtual keyboard, both shown in Figure 3-8.

Tap the Cancel button to cancel an e-mail in progress or save it to the Drafts folder

The From line shows the account being used for this e-mail

The title bar shows what's in the Subject line

Tap Send to send an e-mail

The To line holds your intended recipients

Tap Cc/Bcc to add recipients

The Subject line displays the subject of the e-mail

The body holds the e-mail message

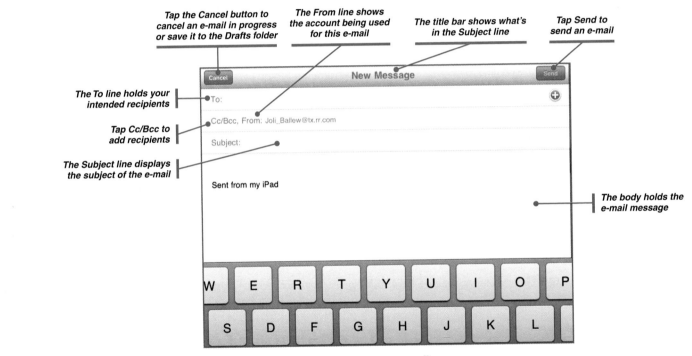

Figure 3-8: *Tap Compose to open a new e-mail.*

To compose a new e-mail:

1. Tap the **Compose** icon.

2. The To: line is active. Tap to type an e-mail address. Tap the **plus sign (+)** to add addresses from your contact list. If you tap the **plus sign (+)**:

   a. Scroll or tap to locate the contact to add.

   b. Tap the **contact name**.

3. To add addresses to the Cc: or Bcc: fields, tap the **Cc/Bcc, From:** line. Repeat step 2 to add additional e-mail addresses.

4. To change the account to send the e-mail from, tap the **Cc/Bcc, From:** line (if you did not tap it in step 3), tap the **email address** shown, and tap a **different account**.

5. Tap the **Subject** line. Enter a subject.

6. Tap in the **Body**. Enter body text.

7. Tap **Send**.

Respond to E-mail

As with other e-mail programs, you can reply to or forward e-mails you receive in Mail. To reply to or forward an e-mail:

1. Tap an e-mail you want to respond to or forward.

2. Click the **Reply/Reply All/Forward/Print** button.

3. Tap **Reply, Reply All**, or **Forward**.

4. Complete the e-mail as desired, and tap **Send**.

E-mail Multiple Photos

You can e-mail a single photo or multiple photos using Mail. You do this from the Photos app, which you'll learn more about in Chapter 4. You can e-mail a single photo from any screen or view in Photos by tapping the **Share** button

---

New M

Cancel   New M   Send

To:

Cc/Bcc, From: Joli_Ballew@tx.rr.com

Subject:

Sent from my iPad

Groups   **All Contacts**

Q Search

A

Jennifer Askew

B

Joli **Ballew**

Lindy **Ballew**

Pico **Ballew**

Xoom **Ballew**

UICKSTEPS

SENDING A TEST E-MAIL

To test your Mail settings, on your iPad, compose and then send a test e-mail for each account you've configured. If you created an account for Gmail, send an e-mail from that account back to that account. And if you've also created an account for Time Warner, send an e-mail from the Time Warner account back to that account too. This will allow you to see if the e-mail accounts are properly configured, how long it takes to receive an e-mail in your inbox once it's been sent, and that the e-mail also arrives on other e-mail–enabled devices you own.

TEST THE ACCOUNTS ON YOUR iPAD

To send a test e-mail:

1. Tap **Mail**.

2. Tap the **Compose** button.

3. Note the address in the From line. This is the account the message will be sent through. Type this address in the To line.

4. In the Subject line, type <u>Test e-mail using my</u> <u>account name account</u>.

SENDING A TEST E-MAIL *(Continued)*

5. Type <u>Test</u> in the body.

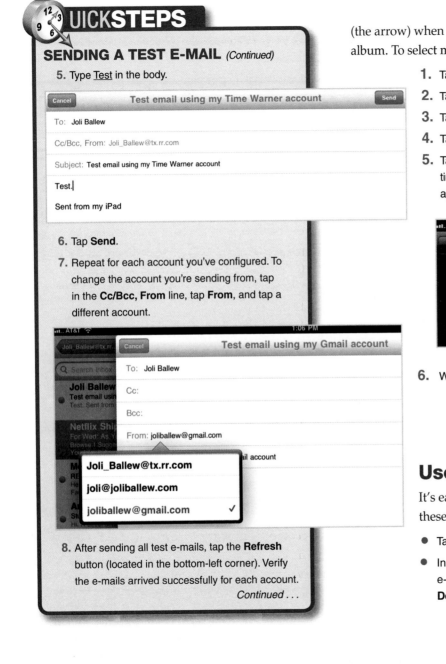

6. Tap **Send**.

7. Repeat for each account you've configured. To change the account you're sending from, tap in the **Cc/Bcc, From** line, tap **From**, and tap a different account.

8. After sending all test e-mails, tap the **Refresh** button (located in the bottom-left corner). Verify the e-mails arrived successfully for each account.

Continued ...

(the arrow) when it appears; but to send multiple photos, you must be in an album. To select multiple photos to e-mail:

1. Tap the **Home** button to access the Home screen.

2. Tap **Photos** and then tap **Albums**.

3. Tap the album that contains the photos you want to send.

4. Tap the arrow in the top-right corner.

5. Tap each photo you want to send. Each time you tap a photo, a check mark will appear on it.

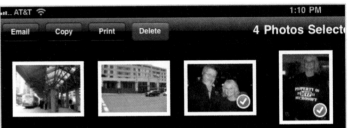

6. When your photos are selected, tap **Email** in the top-left corner.

Use Gestures to Manage E-mail

It's easy to use gestures in Mail, if you know what they are! Perform these gestures and learn how to manage your e-mail with them:

- Tap the **Trash** icon to delete a message.
- In the left pane, flick left or right on any e-mail to access the Delete button. Tap **Delete** if desired.

SENDING A TEST E-MAIL (Continued)

TEST THE ACCOUNTS ON HOME AND WORK COMPUTERS

If you get mail from the same accounts you configured on your iPad on other devices, like home or work computers, iPhones, laptops, and the like, turn off your iPad and test those. From the other devices, perform the same e-mail test detailed earlier and wait for the e-mails you send to arrive back at those devices. Then, turn on your iPad, and verify that you can still receive those test e-mails after they've been downloaded to your other computers and mobile devices. If you do not receive them, refer to the "Reading E-mail Messages on Multiple Devices" QuickFacts earlier in this chapter to learn how to leave a copy of those e-mail messages on the server for each device you own.

NOTE

You can open a Microsoft Word document and read it, but you can't edit that document unless you have a compatible app, such as Apple's Pages. Similar limitations occur with other attachment types.

- Tap **Edit**, tap to select the messages you want to delete, and then tap **Delete**.
- Tap the **Folder** icon to move a message to a different mailbox or folder. Next, navigate to the desired mailbox or folder.
- Tap **Edit**, select the messages you want to move, and tap **Move**.
- **Pinch** your fingers outward to zoom in on a message; pinch inward to zoom out.
- **Double-tap** to zoom out on any zoomed-in message.
- Tap **Details** to see all recipients of a message.
- Tap a **contact's name** to add them to your Contacts list. Tap **Create New Contact** or **Add To Existing Contact** (see Figure 3-9).
- Tap the **blue dot** next to the subject line in the preview pane to mark a message as unread.

Figure 3-9: Add a contact to your Contacts list by tapping their name in an e-mail.

Open an Attachment

Attachments are add-ons to e-mails, and can be pictures, spreadsheets, videos, documents, or even presentations, among other things. You can open many types of attachments on your iPad, although not quite as many as you can on a Mac or a PC. When there's an attachment, you'll see a paperclip.

You can open presentations, documents, and spreadsheets on your iPad by tapping the attachment icon that appears at the bottom of an e-mail. The attachment will open in a new window that enables you to scroll through the attachment, view it, and, if you have a compatible app, edit it. Table 3-1 outlines the compatible attachment types.

QUICKSTEPS

SENDING VIDEOS

You can e-mail video as well as pictures. You may want to e-mail a short video you shot with the Camera app, for instance. Keep in mind when e-mailing video that it must be very short, because you can only attach so much data to an e-mail, and video files are quite large.

1. From the Home screen, tap **Photos**.

2. Locate the video you want to send. If you've taken a video with the Camera app, tap **Albums** and tap **Camera Roll**.

3. Tap the video.

4. Tap the **Forward** button (the arrow).

5. Tap **Email Video**. (Note you can also send this video to YouTube; for more information about video, refer to Chapter 5.)

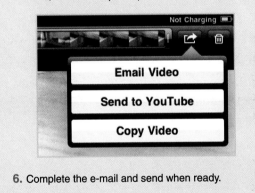

6. Complete the e-mail and send when ready.

FILE EXTENSION	FILE TYPE
.bmp	Bitmap
.doc	Microsoft Word
.docx	Microsoft Word
.htm	webpage
.html	webpage
.jpg	JPEG
.tiff	image
.gif	image
.key	Keynote
.numbers	Numbers
.pages	Pages
.pdf	Preview, Adobe Acrobat
.png	Portable Network Graphics
.ppt	Microsoft PowerPoint
.pptx	Microsoft PowerPoint
.rtf	Rich Text Format
.txt	text document
.vcf	contact information
.xls	Microsoft Excel
.xlsx	Microsoft Excel

Table 3-1: Types of E-mail Attachments That Can Be Opened Using Mail

Pictures behave a little differently from other attached data. You don't have to open pictures separately or get an app. You already have one: Mail. Pictures will automatically appear in the body of an e-mail, and a momentary tap and hold on the image gives you the option to save it or copy it to Photos.

To try to view an attachment represented by a paperclip:

1. Tap **Mail** and tap the e-mail that contains the attachment.

2. Scroll to the bottom of the e-mail and tap the attachment icon.

htde ipad.zip
198 KB

3. To stop viewing the attachment (provided you were able to view it) if it's taking up the entire screen, tap at the top of the document, presentation, or spreadsheet; and then tap **Done**.

4. To save an image in an e-mail to your iPad, tap and hold briefly on the picture, and then tap one of the following options:

    a. **Save Image**

    b. **Save # Images** (this option only appears if there are multiple images)

Search for an E-mail

Sometimes you need to locate an e-mail but can't remember where it is or who it was from, but you do remember what the e-mail was in reference to. In these cases, you can use the Search window to look through your e-mails, using a specific keyword. The more unique the word, the more likely you'll find what you're looking for; performing a search for a less unique word would result in a longer list of search results.

To search for a specific e-mail by keyword using Search:

1. Tap **Mail** and navigate to the account folder you want to search. You may want to select All Inboxes, a single Inbox, a Sent folder, or even an account's Trash folder.

2. Type a keyword into the Search window, above the list of e-mails in the left pane.

3. Review the results, noting you can sort by From, To, Subject, and All.

4. To open any result, tap it.

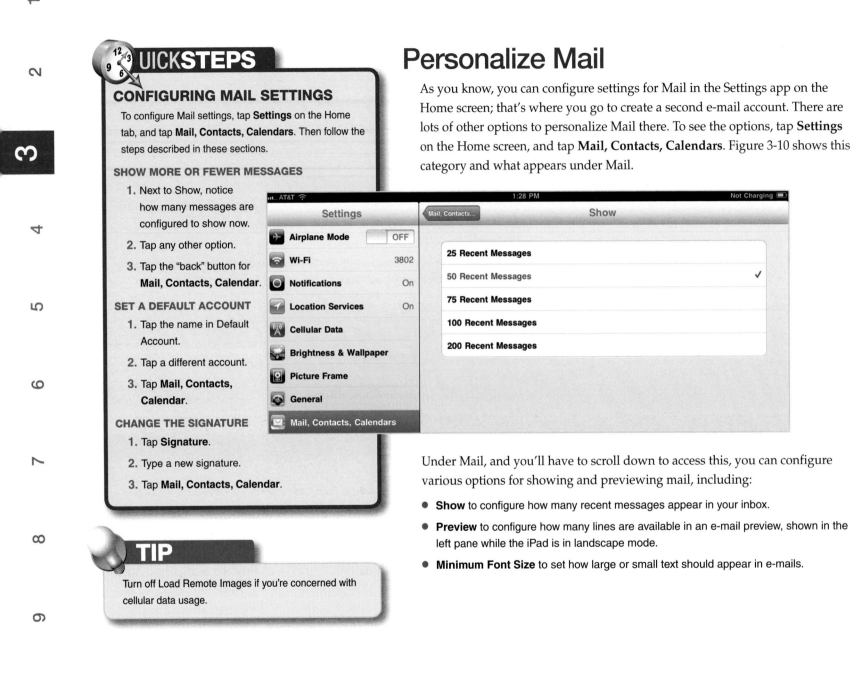

QUICKSTEPS

CONFIGURING MAIL SETTINGS

To configure Mail settings, tap **Settings** on the Home tab, and tap **Mail, Contacts, Calendars**. Then follow the steps described in these sections.

SHOW MORE OR FEWER MESSAGES

1. Next to Show, notice how many messages are configured to show now.

2. Tap any other option.

3. Tap the "back" button for **Mail, Contacts, Calendar**.

SET A DEFAULT ACCOUNT

1. Tap the name in Default Account.

2. Tap a different account.

3. Tap **Mail, Contacts, Calendar**.

CHANGE THE SIGNATURE

1. Tap **Signature**.

2. Type a new signature.

3. Tap **Mail, Contacts, Calendar**.

Personalize Mail

As you know, you can configure settings for Mail in the Settings app on the Home screen; that's where you go to create a second e-mail account. There are lots of other options to personalize Mail there. To see the options, tap **Settings** on the Home screen, and tap **Mail, Contacts, Calendars**. Figure 3-10 shows this category and what appears under Mail.

Under Mail, and you'll have to scroll down to access this, you can configure various options for showing and previewing mail, including:

- **Show** to configure how many recent messages appear in your inbox.
- **Preview** to configure how many lines are available in an e-mail preview, shown in the left pane while the iPad is in landscape mode.
- **Minimum Font Size** to set how large or small text should appear in e-mails.

TIP

Turn off Load Remote Images if you're concerned with cellular data usage.

QUICKFACTS

DISTINGUISHING BETWEEN FETCH AND PUSH

In Settings, under Accounts, next to Fetch New Data is where you configure the *Push* or *Fetch* option. In order to understand which one to use, you need to understand their meanings.

PUSH

Push is a technology that allows Internet servers to send information to your iPad as soon as the message is received by your e-mail provider on their servers. Some servers will push e-mail to you, but not all can do this. Supported e-mail providers include MobileMe, Microsoft Exchange, and Yahoo!, but there are others. Be aware that using Push will require battery power and will minimize battery life. Transfers while connected via 3G are counted toward your monthly data usage as well, so you might not want to enable Push if you are often on a 3G network and away from Wi-Fi. This isn't a problem if you have unlimited access, of course, but it can be if you have a limited plan.

FETCH

Many e-mail accounts such as POP, IMAP, AOL, and Gmail accounts aren't Push-compatible on the iPad. This means that no e-mail will arrive at your inbox in Mail until you open Mail and access it. At that time, Mail will check for e-mail and obtain it from the e-mail servers. If this is inconvenient and you'd rather have Mail check for e-mail automatically, even when you aren't using it, you can configure your iPad to fetch your e-mail on a schedule, every 15, 30, or 60 minutes. You can also set Fetch settings to "Manually" so that no fetch occurs by default. As with Push, Fetch will cause your battery to drain more quickly. To maximize battery life, fetch less often or fetch manually. Fetch also

Continued . . .

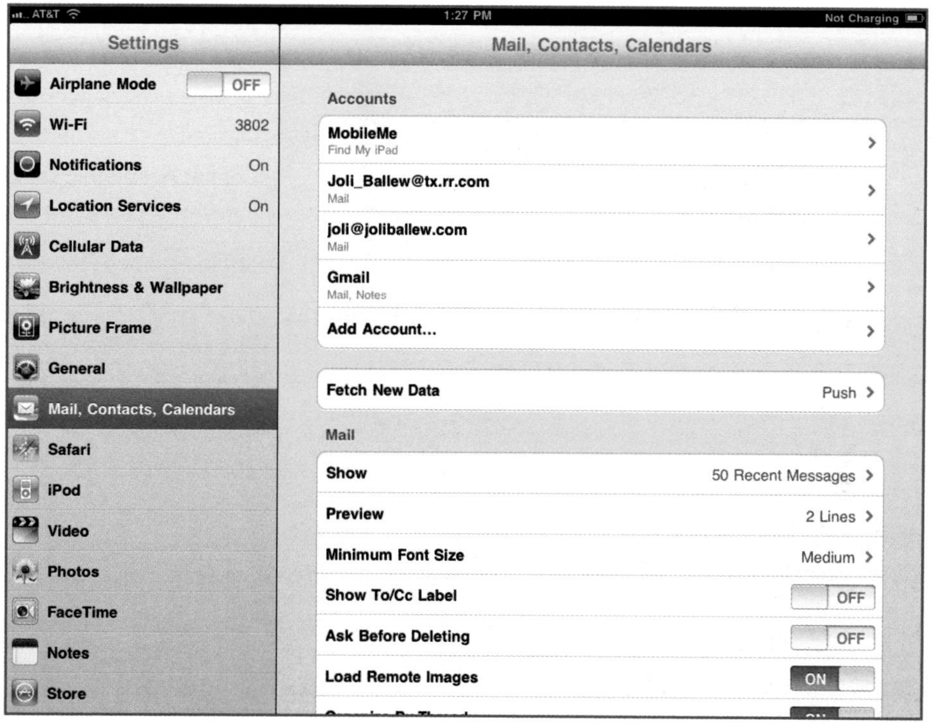

Figure 3-10: The Settings app offers a Mail, Contacts, Calendars category where you can personalize Mail in many ways, including how many messages to show or the minimum font size.

- **Show To/Cc Label** to show or hide the To/Cc label when composing a new e-mail.
- **Ask Before Deleting** to confirm or not confirm the deletion of e-mails.
- **Load Remote Images** to either load or not load images at the same time you load an e-mail.
- **Organize By Thread** to view e-mails by conversations instead of by the time an e-mail arrives.

QUICKFACTS

DISTINGUISHING BETWEEN FETCH AND PUSH (Continued)

kicks in for Push e-mail accounts if Push is turned off, so if you're watching your data usage, you may need to turn off Push and set Fetch to Manual.

To make a choice and configure settings in the Settings app:

1. Tap **Mail, Contacts, Calendars.**

2. Tap **Fetch** or **Push**, whatever is shown next to Fetch New Data.

3. Make your choices as desired.

- **Always Bcc Myself** to either always send a copy of the e-mail to yourself or not.

- **Signature** to add and/or configure a signature for all outgoing e-mails. A signature appears at the bottom of the e-mail. By default, the included signature is "Sent from my iPad."

- **Default Account** to set which account will be used by default when sending photos from the Photo app and when launching e-mails from other apps.

You'll learn about the rest of the available settings in Chapter 10.

Settings	Fetch New Data
Airplane Mode — OFF	
Wi-Fi — 3802	**Push** — ON
Notifications — On	New data will be pushed to your iPad from the server.
Location Services — On	**Fetch**
Cellular Data	The schedule below is used when push is off or for applications which do not support push. For better battery life, fetch less frequently.
Brightness & Wallpaper	
Picture Frame	**Every 15 Minutes**
General	**Every 30 Minutes**
Mail, Contacts, Calendars	**Hourly**
Safari	**Manually** ✓
iPod	
Video	**Advanced** >
Photos	
FaceTime	
Notes	
Store	

How to...

Chapter 4

Using the Camera, Displaying Photos, Viewing Videos, and Exploring FaceTime

The iPad comes with two built-in cameras that you can use to take pictures and shoot videos, and there's a lens on the front and one on the back. The Photos app complements the camera and enables you to view the photos and videos you've taken. You can also upload photos from a camera or Secure Digital (SD) camera card (with an optional adapter), share photos via e-mail, and even print them if you have a compatible printer. If you've taken videos with the camera or uploaded them from another camera or SD card, you can view those too and upload them to YouTube.

On a similar note, the Videos app offers the ability to view videos you purchase, rent, or obtain, including movies, music videos, podcasts, iTunes U media, and other video data. While playing a video, you'll also have easy access to controls that enable you to pause, fast-forward, and rewind the video.

Finally, you can use the camera to have a video chat with another person who has a compatible device, using an app that's included, called FaceTime.

In this chapter you'll learn how to use the camera, use the Photos and Videos apps to view and manage media, view photos in a slideshow, hold a video conversation, and more. You'll learn a little more about syncing too, because syncing all of the media you keep on your computer, purchase, or otherwise obtain can quickly fill up your iPad; you need to know how to sync only data you need to help manage what's on your iPad at any given time.

Use the Camera

You're probably anxious to take a picture! You do that using the Camera app, available from the Home screen. The Camera app is shown in Figure 4-1. There are only a few things to notice: the icon for the last picture taken, the button to take a picture, the switch to move from the photo camera to the video camera, and the option to switch from the back-facing lens to the front or vice versa.

Take a Picture with the Camera

The Camera app is new to the iPad 2, and was not included with the first generation iPad. Since you likely have little or no experience with the iPad 2's

Tap to switch between the front- and rear-facing cameras

Tap to access the Photo app and to view the last picture taken

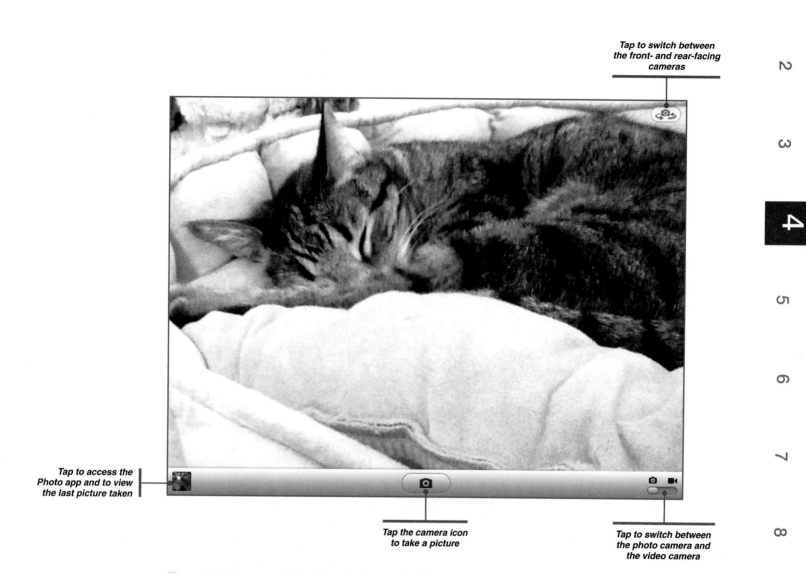

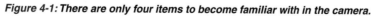

Tap the camera icon to take a picture

Tap to switch between the photo camera and the video camera

Figure 4-1: There are only four items to become familiar with in the camera.

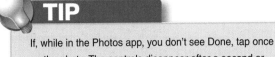

TIP

If, while in the Photos app, you don't see Done, tap once on the photo. The controls disappear after a second or two of idle time.

camera, it's important to learn how to take a picture quickly; you never know when the perfect shot is going to present itself!

1. Tap the camera icon on the Home screen.

2. If applicable, tap the camera icon in the top-right corner to switch to the front- or rear-facing camera.

3. If applicable, tap the camera icon in the bottom-right corner to select the photo camera.

4. Aim, and tap the screen once to let the camera focus in on the shot, if desired. This is optional.

5. Tap the camera icon in the middle of the bottom of the screen to take the picture.

6. To view the picture in the Photos app, tap the thumbnail in the bottom-left corner.

7. Tap **Done** when you're finished viewing the picture. Later, you'll learn how to e-mail a photo, view a slideshow, and more.

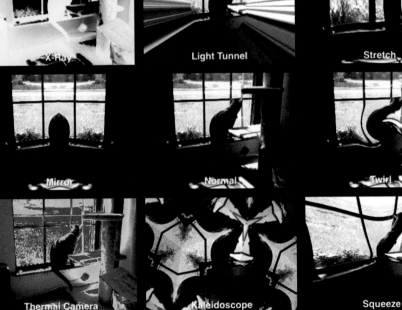

Take a Picture with Photo Booth

The Photo Booth app lets you apply and manipulate effects prior to taking a picture of your subject. There are nine effects in total, including but not limited to X-Ray, Twirl, Thermal Camera, and Kaleidoscope. Once you've taken a few photos, you can view them in full-screen mode and delete them easily, as well as e-mail and copy them.

1. Tap **Photo Booth**.

2. Tap the effect you like.

3. The camera opens. In this window, drag your finger across the screen to apply additional effects. (This won't work if you chose Normal in step 2.)

4. Tap the camera icon to take the picture (this is not shown).

5. To return to Photo Booth to choose a different effect, tap the effect icon in the bottom-left corner, shown in Figure 4-2; to switch camera lenses, tap the camera rotation icon in the bottom-right corner; to view the pictures you've taken, tap any thumbnail, also shown in Figure 4-2.

6. Tap any thumbnail to view it. Flick left and right to view the photos you've taken.

7. Tap the screen again to bring up the controls and thumbnails.

8. Tap any thumbnail and tap the **X** by it to delete it. Tap **Delete Photo**.

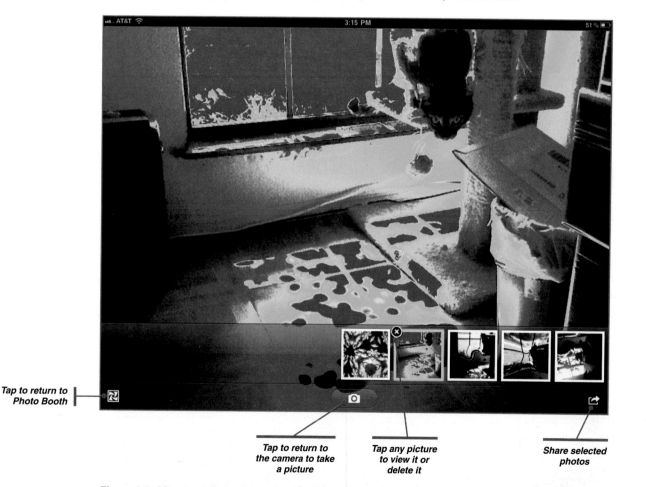

Tap to return to
Photo Booth

Tap to return to
the camera to take
a picture

Tap any picture
to view it or
delete it

Share selected
photos

Figure 4-2: After you take a picture, you'll have options as to what you can do next.

9. To stop viewing photos and return to the camera, tap the camera icon in the middle of the bottom of the screen. (Tap the screen to show this if it's hidden.)

10. To e-mail a photo you've taken (see Figure 4-3):

   a. Tap a photo you want to send.

   b. Tap the arrow that appears in the bottom right of the screen when in thumbnail view.

   c. Tap any additional thumbnails to add photos.

   d. Tap **Email**. (Note you can also copy the photos to paste them somewhere else or cancel the operation.)

   e. Complete the e-mail as desired.

Figure 4-3: Select multiple photos, then tap Email to share them with someone quickly.

Take a Video

You may already know how to record video; it's intuitive, especially if you have already used the camera to take digital pictures. For the most part, you simply select the front- or rear-facing camera, make sure the slider is set to video mode, and tap the **Record** button that appears when the video camera is enabled. Tap the **Record** button again to stop recording. Figure 4-4 shows these controls.

Tap to view the last recorded video

Tap to record video; tap again to stop recording

Tap to select the video camera

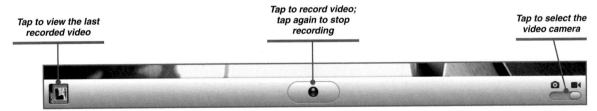

Figure 4-4: Recording is as simple as tapping the Record button.

As with taking digital pictures, a thumbnail appears after you've recorded some video. Tap it to view the recording (and share it) in the Photos app. Keep reading to learn more about the Photos app.

Explore the Photos App

The Photos app enables you to view and share photos and videos with others easily. This app offers features that enable you to send photos in e-mails as detailed in Chapter 3, but you can also assign a photo to a contact, print a photo, or use a photo as wallpaper, among other things. As with other apps, you can employ touch techniques too. When showing your photos, you can flick from left to right to move through photos, flip the entire device to share a photo with someone sitting across from you, and tap and pinch to open an image in full-screen view or zoom in on one. You can easily change views from portrait to landscape view by turning the device 90 degrees left or right. You can even use your iPad as a digital photo frame with Picture Frame, and create your own slideshows of pictures with music from the Photos app.

To open the Photos app, just tap **Photos** on the Home screen. Photos will open, and you'll see two tabs across the top of the page: Photos and Albums. You may also see tabs for Events, Faces, and Places if your photos have relevant, embedded information your iPad can classify into these categories. Figure 4-5 shows the Photos app with the Photos tab selected.

Figure 4-5: The Photos app offers tabs that are related to the photo data you've acquired.

Note what's available in the Photos interface. Specifically, note which of the five tabs are available to you:

- **Photos** is used to view thumbnails of all of your photos and videos individually, and to scroll through the thumbnails by flicking. Tap any photo to view it in full-screen view, or tap any video to play it.

TIP

If you don't have any photos on your iPad, refer to Chapter 1 to sync some using your computer, or you can upload some from a digital camera or SD card as detailed here.

3:53 PM

Photos   Albums   Events   **Places**

- **Albums** is used to view your photos by album name. Use this tab to view your photos by albums. Some albums are created by default by Photos, like Camera Roll and Photos. If you purchase the optional Camera Connection Kit and upload photos using it, you'll see Last Import and All Imported as well. You'll see other folders too, because an album can also be something you create on your computer to organize your own photos. When you sync the pictures you have in folders from your computer, you sync their respective folders to your iPad too. **Events** is available if you sync your iPad with a Mac and use iPhoto or Aperture to organize and manage your photos. You may also see an Events tab even if you don't sync your iPad with a Mac, provided you've somehow acquired photos on your iPad that it can classify as an event.

- **Faces** is available if you use a Mac and iPhoto or Aperture to organize and manage your photos using the built-in face recognition feature. Faces lets you mark a person's face with a name, and then Photos can sort photos by a person, based on the information about their face.

- **Places** is available if you acquire photos on your iPad that contain metadata with information about where they've been taken. If you've uploaded or synced photos taken with a GPS-enabled camera or iPhone, you may see results in the Places tab.

Upload Photos from an SD Card or Camera

There are several ways to copy (upload) pictures from your camera or camera phone to your iPad. You can copy those pictures to your computer and then sync your iPad (see Chapter 1). You can e-mail them from the device (if applicable) to your e-mail address and then save them to your iPad using Mail (see Chapter 3). You can also connect the optional SD Camera Connection Kit or SD card reader and upload them using Photos (read on). The latter is the easiest if you have compatible hardware.

TIP

To order additional components like the Camera Connection Kit, visit www.store.apple.com, and click **Shop iPad**. Scroll to the bottom of the page to view the available accessories.

If you've purchased the Camera Connection Kit, to upload pictures currently on an SD card or on the camera itself:

1. Connect the Camera Connection Kit adapter to the iPad via the 30-pin port at the bottom.

2. Then do one of the following:

   a. Turn on your digital camera and position any settings for playback on that camera, as warranted, and connect the camera to the adapter using the camera's USB cable.

   b. Insert the camera's SD card into the adapter.

3. Tap the **Home** key to wake the iPad, if necessary.

4. Wait while the pictures are read.

5. Tap the pictures you'd like to import. Tap **Import**.

6. Tap **Import All** or **Import Selected**.

7. When the import process has completed, either tap **Delete** to delete the imported media from the camera or **Keep** to keep it.

Use Touch Techniques to View Photos

You view any photo in full-screen view by tapping it once inside the Photos app. To get to the photo you want, you may have to tap the **Photos**, **Albums**, **Events**, or **Places** tab first, or you may have to use the Photos app's "back" button to return to a screen that offers access if you've drilled into a folder to view a picture. The name of this button will change depending on the part of the folder hierarchy you're in.

When you tap a thumbnail of a photo, it appears in a full screen. Figure 4-6 shows this screen. What you see here depends on the photo you're viewing; you won't always see all the icons shown in Figure 4-6 (specifically the options to rotate and delete the photo). Whatever icons you see will disappear in three or four seconds if you don't use them. You can tap once on the photo to bring them back. Thumbnails of the other photos in the album you're viewing appear across the bottom (not shown), and you can tap any thumbnail or slide your finger across them to skip to another photo quickly.

TIP

You can't rotate a picture that's stored in the Camera Roll folder, and you won't see the option to rotate pictures or delete them if you've synced from your computer. But, you can rotate photos you've imported with the Camera Connection Kit. You also can't rotate video.

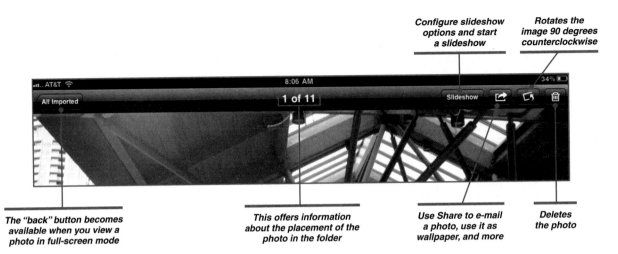

Configure slideshow options and start a slideshow

Rotates the image 90 degrees counterclockwise

The "back" button becomes available when you view a photo in full-screen mode

This offers information about the placement of the photo in the folder

Use Share to e-mail a photo, use it as wallpaper, and more

Deletes the photo

Figure 4-6: When viewing a photo, tap once to show the controls shown here (you won't see all controls in all instances).

NOTE

If you subscribe to MobileMe, you'll see a MobileMe option in various places on your iPad, including under the Share button in Photos.

TIP

You can connect your iPad to an external display, such as a TV or projector, to better share your slideshow with others.

TIP

To stop playing a slideshow, tap the screen.

You can use various touch techniques to view photos, including using a tap, flick, or pinch and physically repositioning the iPad. To view photos using touch techniques:

- **Tap a thumbnail** to view the photo in full-screen view.
- **Tap a picture** in full-screen mode to view the icons and to return to the previous page, print, e-mail, or perform other tasks. Tap again to hide these controls.
- **Reverse-pinch** to zoom in on a photo or to open any folder of photos.
- **Flick** right to left, left to right, top to bottom, or bottom to top to move around in a screen that is longer than one page or to move from photo to photo when viewing pictures in full-screen mode. You can also flick if you've zoomed in on a photo.
- **Double-tap** to zoom in on and then zoom out of a photo.

Copy a Photo

There are many reasons why you would want to copy a photo, but you'll probably want to paste it into the body of an e-mail or a compatible app. You may have apps that allow you to paste into them such as iWork apps like Pages, Numbers, and Keynote.

TIP

You can show any slideshow (or any photo or album) that's on your iPad on an Apple TV if you're connected to your home network via Wi-Fi *and* if the required hardware is available on that network. This works automatically through your Wi-Fi network, with no setup needed. Tap the AirPlay icon to start the show. (Alternately, you can physically connect to your HDTV using the Apple Digital AV Adapter to share a slideshow.)

QUICKSTEPS

CREATING AND VIEWING A SLIDESHOW

There are two ways to enjoy a slideshow of photos. You can create and view a slideshow in the Photos app when your iPad is unlocked, or you can show a slideshow with Picture Frame while your iPad is locked. Picture Frame is an option from the Lock screen, allowing you to offer a slideshow without opening up access to your iPad.

CREATE A SLIDESHOW

To create a slideshow in the Photos app:

1. Tap **Photos**, tap **Album** (you may have to tap a "back" button first), and tap an album you'd like to display in a slideshow. Alternately, tap the **Photos** tab to use all of your photos.

2. Tap **Slideshow**.

Continued . . .

To copy a photo:

1. In Photos, locate the picture you want to copy.

2. Tap the photo to view it in full-screen view.

3. Tap and hold on the screen, and tap **Copy** when it appears.

4. Open an app that supports the Paste command and can accept photos (Notes can't). For example, you can open a new Mail message.

5. Tap and hold, and tap **Paste** when applicable.

Print a Photo

To print from the Photos app, you must have a compatible AirPrint printer available. AirPrint works with other apps too, including Safari, Mail, iWork, PDFs in iBooks, and more. To print from Photos, tap the **Share** icon, and tap **Print**.

Explore the Videos App

The Videos app is where you watch music videos, movies, and TV shows you purchase or rent from iTunes, and movies you've synced from your computer. You can also watch video you've downloaded from iTunes U, video podcasts, and other kinds of media. The Videos app supports high-definition and standard-definition videos and movies, supports closed captioning, and can be viewed in widescreen mode, among other things. Most of the tabs in the Videos app, like the tabs in the Photos app, only appear if you have related types of media.

You may see these tabs in the Videos app:

- **Movies** holds movies you've purchased or rented.
- **TV Shows** holds TV shows you've acquired. You won't see this tab if you don't have any TV shows.
- **Podcasts** holds video podcasts you've acquired. You won't see this tab if you haven't downloaded any video podcasts.
- **Music Videos** holds music videos you've purchased from iTunes. You won't see this tab if you don't have any music videos.
- **iTunes U** holds media obtained from iTunes U. You won't see this tab if you don't have any iTunes U media.

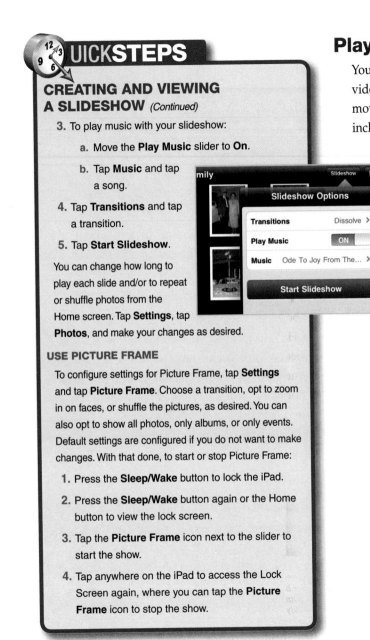

QUICKSTEPS

CREATING AND VIEWING A SLIDESHOW (Continued)

3. To play music with your slideshow:

  a. Move the **Play Music** slider to **On**.

  b. Tap **Music** and tap a song.

4. Tap **Transitions** and tap a transition.

5. Tap **Start Slideshow**.

You can change how long to play each slide and/or to repeat or shuffle photos from the Home screen. Tap **Settings**, tap **Photos**, and make your changes as desired.

USE PICTURE FRAME

To configure settings for Picture Frame, tap **Settings** and tap **Picture Frame**. Choose a transition, opt to zoom in on faces, or shuffle the pictures, as desired. You can also opt to show all photos, only albums, or only events. Default settings are configured if you do not want to make changes. With that done, to start or stop Picture Frame:

1. Press the **Sleep/Wake** button to lock the iPad.

2. Press the **Sleep/Wake** button again or the Home button to view the lock screen.

3. Tap the **Picture Frame** icon next to the slider to start the show.

4. Tap anywhere on the iPad to access the Lock Screen again, where you can tap the **Picture Frame** icon to stop the show.

Play a Movie

You need to have movies or videos on your iPad to view them. You can obtain video media by syncing it from your computer; you can rent or purchase movies from iTunes; and you can download free podcasts from various places, including iTunes, which is detailed in Chapter 6.

To find and play a video using the Videos app:

1. Tap the Videos app on the Home screen.

2. Tap the tab that contains the media you want to view. Figure 4-7 shows the Movies tab.

3. Tap any video to see more information.

4. Tap **Play**.

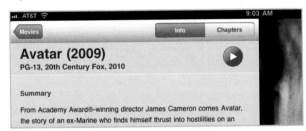

Figure 4-7: If you have compatible media on your iPad, it'll appear under its related tab in the Videos app.

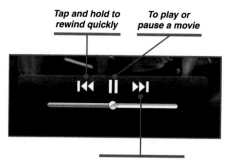

USING PHOTOS FOR CONTACTS AND WALLPAPER

Any picture on your iPad can be assigned to a contact or used as wallpaper. Contacts are detailed in Chapter 8, and hold information about people you communicate with. Wallpaper is the picture you see when your iPad is locked, as well as the picture you see on any Home screen.

ASSIGN A PHOTO TO A CONTACT

To assign a photo to a contact:

1. Tap **Photos**.
2. Tap the photo you want to use.
3. Tap the **Share** button.
4. Tap **Assign To Contact**.
5. Tap the desired contact.
6. If desired, move and scale the image by dragging your finger on it.
7. Tap **Use**.

SET A PHOTO AS WALLPAPER

To set a photo as wallpaper:

1. Tap **Photos**.
2. Tap the photo you want to use.
3. Tap the **Share** button.
4. Tap **Use As Wallpaper**.
5. Tap **Set Lock Screen**, **Set Home Screen**, or **Set Both**.

If you record video with a digital camera and upload that video to your iPad with the optional Camera Connection Kit or media card reader, iPad-compatible videos will appear in the Photos app, not the Videos app.

Use Video Controls

When watching a movie, you'll have controls available to you. To use the video controls while watching a movie:

1. Tap the screen.
2. Tap any control to apply it (see Figures 4-8 and 4-9).
3. Tap the screen to hide the controls. They will disappear automatically after about six seconds. Tap again to make those controls reappear.

Figure 4-8: The controls let you control the movie.

Sync Only Specific Photos or Videos

You learned a little about syncing in Chapter 1, and you'll learn even more in Chapter 10. However, it's important to address syncing media here as well, because media takes up lots of storage space and can easily fill your iPad with data you don't want or need. The best way to handle this storage issue is to sync often and review what

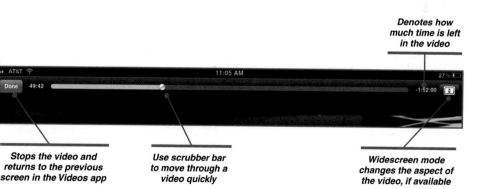

Figure 4-9: These controls help you navigate the movie.

you're syncing regularly. Remove movies you've seen and store them on your computer, and only store movies you haven't seen or plan to watch again soon on your iPad.

1. Connect your iPad to your computer with the USB cable.
2. In iTunes, in the left pane, click your iPad.
3. In iTunes, click **Movies**.
4. Click **Sync Movies**.
5. Deselect, if applicable, **Automatically Include**.
6. Select only the media you want to sync.
7. Repeat with other applicable categories, such as TV Shows, iTunes U, or others.
8. Click **Apply**.

Note that there are additional options in iTunes. You can select Automatically Include, for instance, and select an option such as All Unwatched, 5 Most Recent, and other options. You can deselect this option and choose to sync media you've purchased on your computer or your iPad.

HAVING A VIDEO CHAT WITH FACETIME

To conduct a video chat using FaceTime:

1. Tap **FaceTime** on the Home screen.

2. If this is your first time using FaceTime, provide your Apple ID and password, tap **Next**, and verify the e-mail address (or type a new one). Tap **Done**.

3. In the All Contacts list that appears, tap the contact you want to send a FaceTime invitation to. If the contact has a blue camera by their name, they're available for FaceTime and have the required hardware.

4. Tap that e-mail address to initiate the call. A call in progress offers controls to switch from the front- to the rear-facing camera, to mute the sound, and to end the conversation.

TIP

Tap **Settings** and tap **FaceTime** to change or add an e-mail address, or to turn FaceTime on or off.

Explore FaceTime

FaceTime is an app that lets you hold video chats with others. People you want to video-chat with must have an iPad 2, iPhone 4, new iPod touch, or a Mac over Wi-Fi. They must have FaceTime set up as well, which only consists of two steps. They have to provide an Apple ID and password, and provide or verify the e-mail address they want to associate with it.

Because calls are placed by tapping a contact's e-mail address, when you first tap FaceTime, you'll be prompted to provide your own Apple ID and password, and then tell FaceTime what e-mail address you want to use when people call you. With that done, FaceTime is ready to use.

Chapter 5

Getting and Listening to Music and Audio

You play music on your iPad with the iPod app. This app is positioned at the bottom of your iPad, and allows you to access the music on your iPad, play it, and view album art and track information. While playing music, you'll have access to familiar controls, like pause, rewind, and repeat, and some that you may not be so familiar with, like shuffle and Genius. You can use the iPod to create playlists, sort your music, and search for specific music by its attributes too.

In this chapter you'll learn how to use the iPod app. First, you'll need to obtain some music. You can sync music already stored on your computer, detailed here, or you can refer to Chapter 6 to learn how to purchase music from iTunes.

NOTE

For the most part, in this chapter we'll focus on music. However, you can listen to and control audiobooks, podcasts, and music videos in the same manner and using the same controls.

TIP

Currently, you can't drag and drop music from your computer to your iPad without using iTunes, but if that's something you'd like to do, watch for upcoming third-party apps. This feature would come in handy if you were at a friend's house, for example, and wanted to copy some of their music but didn't want to use iTunes.

CAUTION

Choose one computer, and use that one computer to sync your iPad every time. Do not attempt to sync your iPad with more than one computer, as data loss may occur.

TIP

If you don't have any music on your computer, insert a music CD, and when prompted, opt to import songs using iTunes.

Obtain Music

There are two main ways to get music onto your iPad. The first is to use iTunes and your computer to copy (sync) music you already own to your iPad. The music on your computer is often music you've ripped from the CDs you own, or music you've purchased from the iTunes store using iTunes on your computer (and have yet to sync to your iPad). The second is to use the iTunes app on the iPad to buy music from the iTunes Store and download it directly to your iPad. When syncing with your computer, you can opt to sync your entire music library or just specific playlists, artists, and/or genres. Each time you acquire music, either from your iPad or on your computer, it can be synced too, so your music libraries will always be up-to-date.

Sync Personal Music Files

To copy music that is on your computer to your iPad, you connect your iPad to your computer and set up syncing. Once syncing is set up, any changes made to either music library (on the iPad or the computer) are automatically synced each time you connect the two devices. It is best to put all of your music on one computer (the computer you used to activate your iPad), and use that computer to copy, manage, and sync music between the two.

To sync music from your PC to your iPad using iTunes (performing this on a Mac is similar):

1. Connect your iPad to your computer.
2. In the source pane in iTunes, on your computer, click the icon for your iPad.
3. Click the **Music** tab (see Figure 5-1).
4. Select the desired syncing options.
5. If desired, select **Automatically Fill Free Space With Songs**. You may want to do this if you've synced specific music files because your entire music library won't fit on your iPad, but you'd like to have as much music as possible available on it.
6. Click **Sync**.

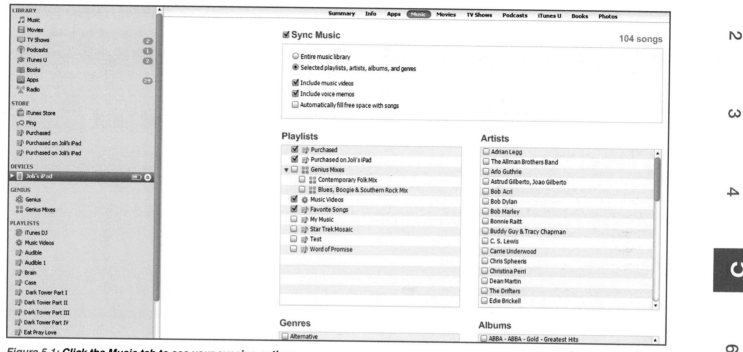

Figure 5-1: *Click the Music tab to see your syncing options.*

NOTE

Once syncing is set up, it will occur automatically each time you connect your iPad to your computer.

Sync Audiobooks

You can get audiobooks from the iTunes Store, detailed in Chapter 6. If you have an audiobook already, either one you've purchased or one you've synced from your computer, you can find it and listen to it using the iPod app on the iPad. For more information on purchasing and downloading audiobooks from iTunes, refer to that chapter. Your iPad also supports *Audible* files (Audible is one of the largest audiobook companies in the world). In addition to audiobooks, Audible .com offers magazines; radio shows; podcasts; stand-up comedy; and speeches from people who shape culture, politics, and business.

If you have any audiobooks, you can sync them in the same manner as you sync music. Connect your iPad to your computer, select your iPad in the source pane

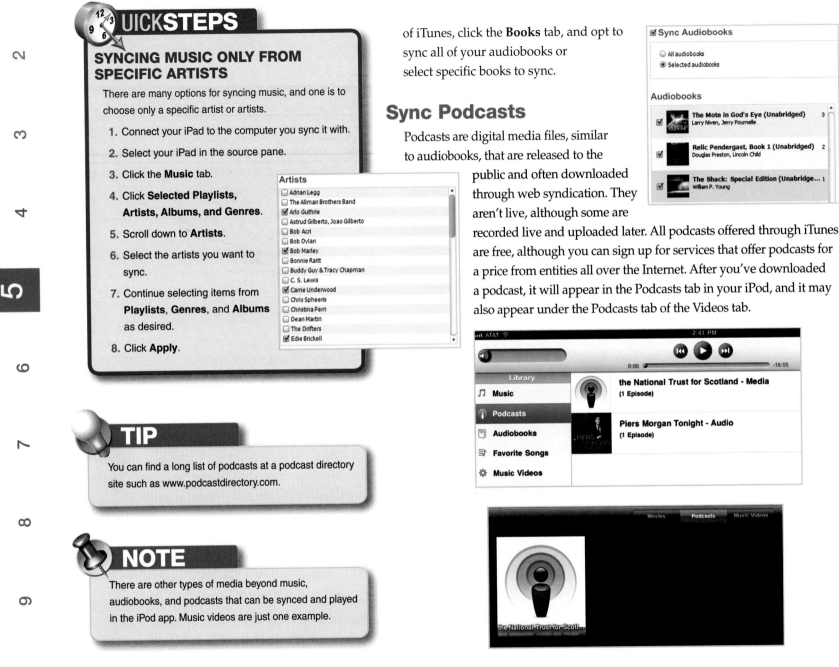

SYNCING MUSIC ONLY FROM SPECIFIC ARTISTS

There are many options for syncing music, and one is to choose only a specific artist or artists.

1. Connect your iPad to the computer you sync it with.

2. Select your iPad in the source pane.

3. Click the **Music** tab.

4. Click **Selected Playlists, Artists, Albums, and Genres**.

5. Scroll down to **Artists**.

6. Select the artists you want to sync.

7. Continue selecting items from **Playlists**, **Genres**, and **Albums** as desired.

8. Click **Apply**.

Artists
- ☐ Adrian Legg
- ☐ The Allman Brothers Band
- ☑ Arlo Guthrie
- ☐ Astrud Gilberto, Joao Gilberto
- ☐ Bob Acri
- ☐ Bob Dylan
- ☑ Bob Marley
- ☐ Bonnie Raitt
- ☐ Buddy Guy & Tracy Chapman
- ☐ C. S. Lewis
- ☑ Carrie Underwood
- ☐ Chris Spheeris
- ☐ Christina Perri
- ☐ Dean Martin
- ☐ The Drifters
- ☑ Edie Brickell

TIP

You can find a long list of podcasts at a podcast directory site such as www.podcastdirectory.com.

NOTE

There are other types of media beyond music, audiobooks, and podcasts that can be synced and played in the iPod app. Music videos are just one example.

---

of iTunes, click the **Books** tab, and opt to sync all of your audiobooks or select specific books to sync.

☑ Sync Audiobooks

○ All audiobooks
● Selected audiobooks

Audiobooks

- ☑ **The Mote in God's Eye (Unabridged)**   3
  Larry Niven, Jerry Pournelle
- ☑ **Relic Pendergast, Book 1 (Unabridged)**   2
  Douglas Preston, Lincoln Child
- ☑ **The Shack: Special Edition (Unabridge...**   1
  William P. Young

Sync Podcasts

Podcasts are digital media files, similar to audiobooks, that are released to the public and often downloaded through web syndication. They aren't live, although some are recorded live and uploaded later. All podcasts offered through iTunes are free, although you can sign up for services that offer podcasts for a price from entities all over the Internet. After you've downloaded a podcast, it will appear in the Podcasts tab in your iPod, and it may also appear under the Podcasts tab of the Videos tab.

atll AT&T   2:41 PM

0:00 ———————— -18:55

Library

- ♫ Music
- ⦿ Podcasts
- ▤ Audiobooks
- ▤ Favorite Songs
- ✿ Music Videos

the National Trust for Scotland - Media
(1 Episode)

Piers Morgan Tonight - Audio
(1 Episode)

Movies   Podcasts   Music Videos

the National-Trust-for-Scotl...

Browse Music

To play music on your iPad, you open the iPod app, browse for the media you want to play, and tap it to play it. You can browse for media in many ways: by songs, artists, albums, genres, and composers; or you can search for something by typing a song name, artist name, or other metadata. Depending on the media you've synced or acquired, you may also be able to browse categories including podcasts, purchased, playlists by their names, music videos, audiobooks, and more.

Here are a few of the libraries you may see:

- **Music** This library holds all of your music. The default view is Songs, and the songs are listed alphabetically. There are other views available across the bottom: Artists, Albums, Genres, and Composers. Figure 5-2 shows this view.

- **Podcasts** This library only holds media deemed by the iPod to be podcasts.

- **Audiobooks** This library only holds media deemed by the iPod to be audiobooks.

- **<Playlists>** These entries under libraries are playlists you've synced from your computer or created in the iPod app.

- **Music Videos** This library holds music videos you've purchased.

- **Purchased and Purchased On** Entries that start with the word Purchased hold media you've purchased on this device or other iDevices you own. If you have more than one entry for Purchased, you've synced media from other iDevices to your iPad through iTunes.

Figure 5-2: *The Music view lists songs alphabetically, but there are additional views.*

Labels around figure:
Volume slider
Rewind, Pause/Play, Fast-Forward
Search
Libraries and Playlists
Genius
New Playlist

Now Playing:
Everlast
Saving Grace (Theme)
Saving Grace (Theme) - Single

R				
River of Tears	Eric Clapton	Clapton Chronicles: Th...	7:21	
Room Full of Mirrors	The Pretenders	Get Close	4:36	
Running on Faith	Eric Clapton	Clapton Chronicles: Th...	6:26	
S				
Safe in My Garden	The Mamas and the...	The Mamas & The Pap...	3:00	
Sapphire	Chris Spheeris	Culture	5:02	
▶ Saving Grace (The...	Everlast	Saving Grace (Theme)...	3:07	
Seven Wonders	Fleetwood Mac	Tango in the Night	3:42	
Shadow of Doubt	Bonnie Raitt	Longing in Their Hearts	4:26	
She	Edie Brickell & New Bo...	Shooting Rubberbands...	5:08	
She's Waiting	Eric Clapton	Clapton Chronicles: Th...	4:58	
Silver Inches	Enya	A Day Without Rain	1:37	
Sleep Away	Bob Acri	Bob Acri	3:20	
Sowing the Seeds...	Tears for Fears	The Seeds of Love	6:19	

Songs | Artists | Albums | Genres | Composers

QUICKSTEPS

EXPLORING THE iPOD CATEGORIES

Make sure you've synced various kinds of music and audio to your iPod. Tap the iPod app to open it.

BROWSE LIBRARIES

1. Under Library, tap **Music**.
2. Note the category at the bottom. If desired, tap a different category.
3. Under Library, tap **Podcasts**, **Audiobooks**, **Purchased**, or any other library.
4. Note any available categories at the bottom. If desired, tap a different category.

BROWSE CATEGORIES

1. Under Library, tap **Music**.
2. At the bottom of the iPod interface, tap **Songs**.
3. Tap **Artists**.
4. Tap **Albums**.
5. Tap **Genres**.
6. Tap **Composers**.

NOTE

You can use Spotlight Search to launch and play music, video, and other files without first launching the associated app.

Finally, across the bottom of the iPod, you'll see the following categories. Tap any category title to change the results:

- **Songs** displays all of the songs on your iPod by title.
- **Artists** displays your music by artist.
- **Albums** displays your albums in alphabetical order.
- **Genres** displays music by genre, such as folk, rock, alternative, and soundtrack, among others.
- **Composers** displays your music according to its composer.

Play Media

Playing a song is one of the simplest things you can do with the iPod. You tap it. Once a song is playing, there are a few things you'll want to do right away, including changing the volume (the volume may be way too loud or muted, as an example).

To adjust the volume with the external controls:

- Locate the **Volume** buttons on the outside of the iPad to increase or decrease the volume.
- Press the Silent/Screen Rotation Lock to mute the music, provided the setting for that is Mute in Settings (it's user-configurable).

Use Media Controls

The iPod app offers controls for playing, pausing, rewinding, fast-forwarding, and changing the volume by touching the controls available on the screen. You saw the controls on the default iPod screen earlier in Figure 5-2. There are other views, however, and each of the views also offers controls. Figure 5-3 shows one such view, where the album art is showing and the controls are available at the top of the page. (At the bottom of the page, not shown, are the options to go back to the previous view, tell Genius to create a Genius playlist based on that song, and change from Album Art view to List view.)

NOTE

While a song is playing, tap the screen to access the iPod controls. You can then move the volume slider on the screen to adjust the volume without using the Volume buttons.

TIP

Purchase AirPlay-enabled speakers for your iPad and stream your music to them, without wires. Once you have the speakers set up, you'll see the AirPlay icon on the iPod app.

QUICKSTEPS

PLAYING AND CONTROLLING AUDIO

Browse to any song to play, and tap it once to play it. By default, Album Art view will appear and no controls will be available on the screen. Now, experiment with the following controls.

PAUSE, STOP, PLAY, AND RESTART

To pause, play, stop, and restart a song:

1. Tap the screen to show the controls.

2. Tap the **Pause** button; it becomes a Play button. The song pauses.

3. Tap the **Play** button to continue playing the song from where it was paused.

4. Drag the scrubber to the far left to restart the song from the beginning.

RETURN TO LIBRARY

1. Tap the **Back To Library** button.

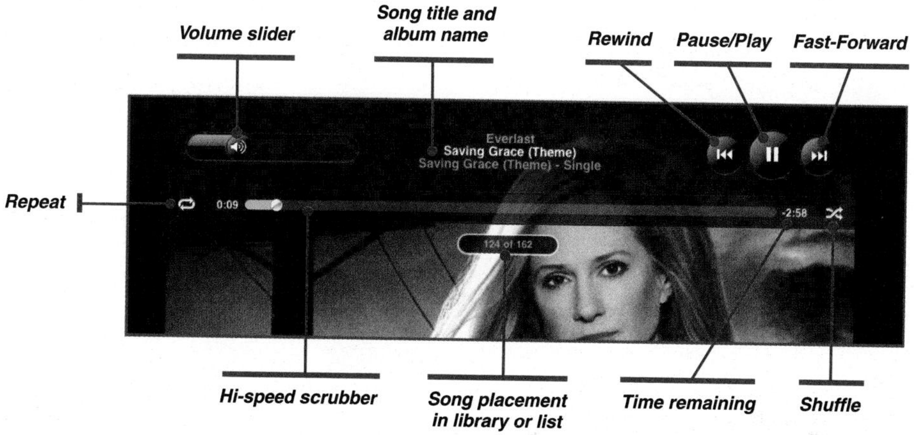

Figure 5-3: *In Album Art view, you can see the album cover and have access to various controls.*

Labels: Volume slider · Song title and album name · Rewind · Pause/Play · Fast-Forward · Repeat · Hi-speed scrubber · Song placement in library or list · Time remaining · Shuffle

Switch Views

When you play a song, you have the option to view the iPod Music Library screen, album art, or information about the album or tracks on the playlist. Album Art is the album cover. The Track View shows the list of songs in an album, among other things. Track View allows you to move among songs in an album or playlist. You're familiar with the default screen already.

Incorporate Playlists

The list of songs on an album is called a playlist; it's a list of songs to be played. You can create your own playlists and add any songs you like to personalize your music experience. In a personalized playlist, you get to handpick the songs to include. There's built-in support for creating playlists in the iPod app. (Depending on your age, you may liken a playlist to an older type of music playlist of songs: the "mixed tape.")

PLAYING AND CONTROLLING
AUDIO *(Continued)*

2. To return to the Album Art view, tap the **Now Playing** icon. As you can see here, not all of your music will have album artwork.

Now Playing:

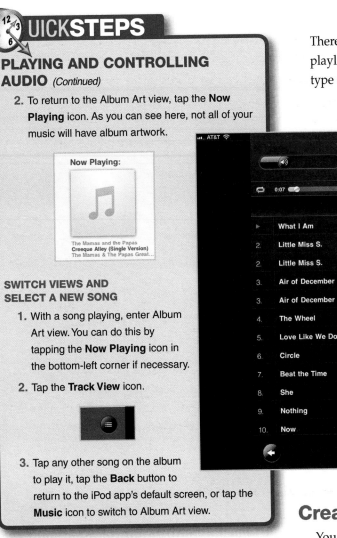

The Mamas and the Papas
Creeque Alley (Single Version)
The Mamas & The Papas Great...

SWITCH VIEWS AND
SELECT A NEW SONG

1. With a song playing, enter Album Art view. You can do this by tapping the **Now Playing** icon in the bottom-left corner if necessary.

2. Tap the **Track View** icon.

3. Tap any other song on the album to play it, tap the **Back** button to return to the iPod app's default screen, or tap the **Music** icon to switch to Album Art view.

NOTE

The iPod app contains a Search feature. If you're looking for a song, audiobook, podcast, or any other item that is in any of your iPod libraries, you can search for it here. When you type something in the search box, the results will appear as you type.

There's another type of playlist you may not be familiar with; it's a *Genius* playlist. Genius analyzes your music library and draws conclusions about what type of list you'll like, based on a song you pick.

▶	What I Am	Edie Brickell & New Bohe...	4:58
2.	Little Miss S.	Edie Brickell & New Bohe...	3:39
2.	Little Miss S.	Edie Brickell & New Bohe...	3:39
3.	Air of December	Edie Brickell & New Bohe...	5:59
3.	Air of December	Edie Brickell & New Bohe...	5:59
4.	The Wheel	Edie Brickell & New Bohe...	3:54
5.	Love Like We Do	Edie Brickell & New Bohe...	3:09
6.	Circle	Edie Brickell & New Bohe...	3:13
7.	Beat the Time	Edie Brickell & New Bohe...	2:58
8.	She	Edie Brickell & New Bohe...	5:08
9.	Nothing	Edie Brickell & New Bohe...	4:51
10.	Now	Edie Brickell & New Bohe...	6:04

Create a Genius Playlist

You can create a Genius playlist by tapping a song you want to base the list on and tapping the Genius icon at the bottom of the screen.

1. Tap **iPod** to open the app.

2. Tap a song to be the basis for the playlist. It will begin to play.

3. With a song playing, tap the **Genius** icon.

Now Playing:

Edie Brickell & New Bohemians
Beat the Time
Shooting Rubberbands at the...

TIP

The best way to view the playlist is to tap **Genius** in the left pane, view the playlists by artists, and then view the playlists by genres.

QUICKSTEPS

CREATING A PERSONALIZED PLAYLIST

A standard, or *personalized*, playlist is a playlist you create by manually selecting the songs you want to include in it. Once created, a playlist can be edited.

CREATE A STANDARD PLAYLIST

To create a standard playlist on your iPad's iPod app:

1. Tap the plus sign (+) sign at the bottom of the iPod interface. This is the Add Playlist button.

2. Type a name for the playlist, and tap **Save**.

3. Tap each song you want to add. It will appear grayed out after you tap it.

4. Tap **Done**.

5. If desired, edit the playlist. You'll learn more about this in the next section.

6. Tap **Done**.

Continued . . .

4. If there is enough information for the iPod to draw from, a new Genius playlist will be created. You can access this playlist from the Genius tab in the iPod app's Songs view.

5. To save the playlist, tap the **Save** button in the upper-right corner of the screen.

You can also create a Genius playlist from the Genius tab in the iPod app. Just tap **Genius** in the left pane, and in Songs view, tap **New**. Here you can select a single song for Genius to use, and another new playlist will be created.

QUICKSTEPS

CREATING A PERSONALIZED PLAYLIST (Continued)

EDIT A PLAYLIST YOU'VE CREATED

To edit a playlist:

1. Tap the playlist you want to edit, and then tap **Edit**.

2. To move a song up or down in the list, tap, hold, and drag it to the desired location. You must drag from the far right end of the song to the right of the information regarding the song's duration.

3. To delete any song, tap it and tap **Delete**. (Deleting a song from a playlist doesn't delete it from your iPad.)

4. To add more songs, tap **Add Songs**, tap the songs you want to add, and then tap **Done**.

5. Tap **Done** again.

	AT&T	5:00 PM	▶ Not Charging

0:59 ————————————————— -1:47

Library   Sleepy Time Music   **Edit**

- ⓘ Podcasts
- 🗐 Audiobooks
- ✳ Genius
- 🖹 Favorite Songs
- ✿ Music Videos
- 🖹 My Music
- 🖹 Purchased
- 🖹 Purchased on Joli'…
- 🖹 Sleepy Time Music

Now Playing:

Edie Brickell & New Bohemians
Keep Coming Back
Shooting Rubberbands at the…

Shuffle ✂

Air of December	Edie Brickell & New Bo...	Shooting Rubberbands...	5:59
Allura	Chris Spheeris	Culture	5:56
Aria	Chris Spheeris	Culture	4:49
Change the World	Eric Clapton	Clapton Chronicles: The...	3:55
Deora Ar Mo Chroi	Enya	A Day Without Rain	2:48
Elektra	Chris Spheeris	Culture	5:24
Blue Eyes Blue	Eric Clapton	Clapton Chronicles: The...	4:42
Embrace	Chris Spheeris	Culture	4:09
Fallen Embers	Enya	A Day Without Rain	2:31
Fast Car	Tracy Chapman	Tracy Chapman	3:00
Flora's Secret	Enya	A Day Without Rain	4:07

Songs   Artists   Albums   Genres   Composers

If you received a message that Genius playlists are not enabled, at the computer you use to sync your iPad:

1. Connect your iPad to your computer.

2. Click **Genius** from the left pane in iTunes, and then click **Turn On Genius**.

3. Type your password.

4. Read and agree to the terms of service.

5. Wait while Genius compiles the required information.

6. Click your iPad icon in the left pane.

7. Click **Sync**.

NOTE

To quickly shuffle all the songs in your collection, tap the **Music** tab in the iPod app's Songs view, and pull down on the music list to reveal the Shuffle option.

TIP

The icon to the left of the scrubber bar and to the left of the amount of time the song has been playing is the Repeat button. Tap it to repeat the song once it's finished playing (a 1 will appear by it). You can also tap to repeat the song over and over.

TIP

Create a "smart playlist" in iTunes on your computer that contains your top rated or favorite songs. You can also create playlists that contain the songs you play the most. Then, sync that playlist to your iPad. Smart playlists are just that; they're smart and update themselves as your tastes change and as criteria for the playlist is met.

Play a Playlist

You tap a playlist to access it, and tap a song in it to play it. When you play songs in any list, they play from top to bottom, or from start to finish, no matter what the source of the list. You may want to *shuffle* those songs so they play in random order, especially if this list is in alphabetical order or if the songs in the list are grouped by artist or album.

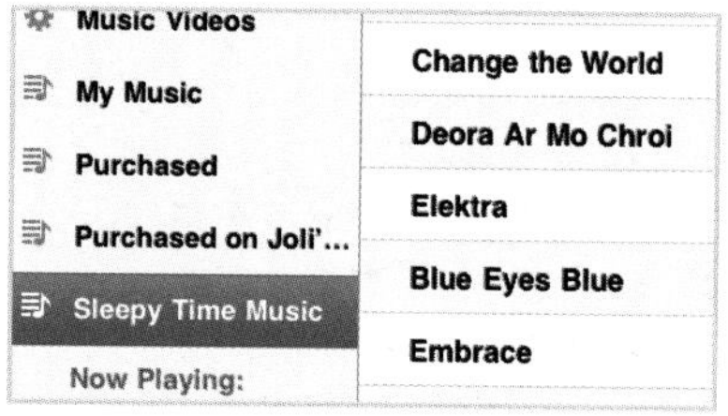

1. Under Library, tap a playlist.
2. Tap any song in the playlist to start playing it.

Sync Playlists

When you connect your iPad to your computer, playlists you've created on your iPad will sync to your iTunes music library on your computer. You'll see the playlist in two places in iTunes: in the source pane under Playlists (not shown), and when your iPad is selected, under the Music tab. Figure 5-4 shows the latter.

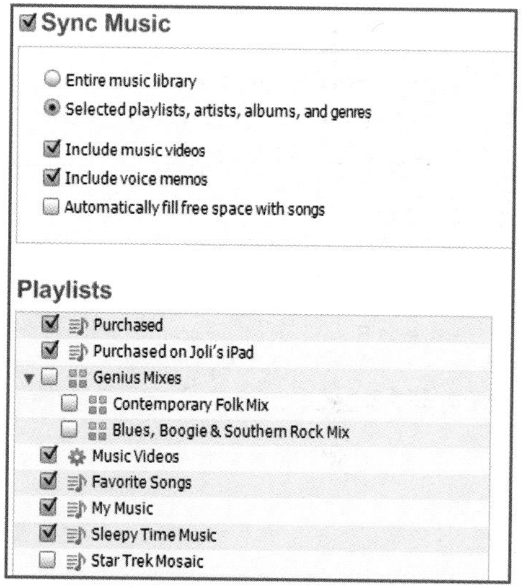

***Figure 5-4:* Playlists you create on your iPad will sync to your iTunes music library.**

You can select only specific playlists to sync under the Music tab. In addition, you can create playlists in iTunes at your computer and include those.

Chapter 6

Shopping iTunes, the App Store, and the iBookstore

You may have music, movies, audiobooks, and other data on your computer that you can sync to your iPad, but you probably don't have apps, podcasts, digital books, the latest music video, or a copy of last week's airing of your favorite TV show (unless you're upgrading from your first iPad to the iPad 2). That's what this chapter is all about: obtaining media from the Internet and putting in on your iPad. You'll also learn how to acquire apps from the App Store and books from the iBookstore. You'll learn all about using the iBooks app to read those books too.

Shop with iTunes

The iTunes you'll use on your iPad is different from the iTunes on your computer. iTunes on your computer is a full-fledged music management program; iTunes on your iPad simply offers access to the iTunes Store. The iTunes Store is a one-stop shop for music, TV shows, movies, podcasts, audiobooks, and even college lectures from universities. You can preview and buy just about any kind of media imaginable. And, like other iPad media, it's easy to sync your newly acquired media to your desktop computer.

Once you've acquired media from the iTunes Store, you'll use other apps to view it or listen to it. You listen to music, podcasts, and audiobooks with the iPod app. You watch movies, music videos, and TV shows with the Videos app. You can watch music videos and listen to media from iTunes U from both the iPod and the Videos app. The iTunes interface is shown in Figure 6-1.

Understand the iTunes Interface

When you enter the iTunes Store (by tapping the iTunes icon on your iPad), you have access to various buttons to help you navigate iTunes. These options help you sort the media by its type and then narrow down the results.

CHOOSE A MEDIA CATEGORY

The categories across the bottom of the page help you navigate iTunes by making sorting options available. Tap any category button to show only media in that category:

- **Music**   Tap to find music and have easy access to music videos and free content on iTunes.

The Genres button narrows
the results shown on
any screen

Featured, Top Charts, and Genius
buttons help you navigate what's
hot and what you might like

The Search window
lets you search for any
media by name

Figure 6-1: *The iTunes interface offers myriad ways to browse media.*

The categories that run across
the bottom of the page
sort media by type

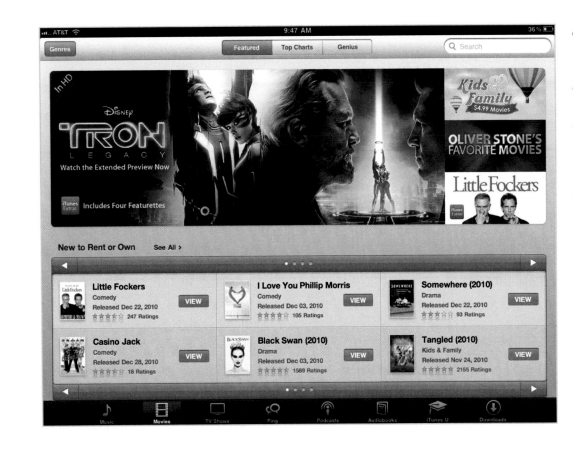

- **Movies** Tap to buy or rent movies, see recent arrivals, and access free movie previews.

- **TV Shows** Tap to locate and purchase entire seasons of shows or single shows.

- **Ping** Tap to view the activities of people you "follow." Tap **People** to choose people to follow, and tap **My Profile** to view what iTunes has deemed important about you.

- **Podcasts** Tap to browse podcasts that are available from the iTunes Store. All podcasts are currently free.

- **Audiobooks** Tap to see what the iTunes Store offers in the way of audiobooks. You can get free audiobooks from iTunes U.

- **iTunes U** Tap to browse college lectures from Yale, Berkeley, and others; browse K-12 offerings; and even watch videos taken in museums and television stations. You can also download free audiobooks.

- **Downloads** Tap to see items related to media you're currently downloading. Once the media has been downloaded, the list will be empty and the media will be available in its associated app.

NARROW DOWN THE RESULTS

Once you're in the desired category, narrow down the results with the available options, or use the Search window to search for something specific. The options available will change depending on the tab you've selected, and you won't see all options on every category screen:

- **Genres/Categories** Tap to show the available genres and categories for the selected media type. What's offered will change depending on what you've selected across the bottom of the screen. For instance, if you're browsing TV shows, then the Genres button produces All, Animation, Classic, Comedy, Drama, Kids, Nonfiction, Reality TV,

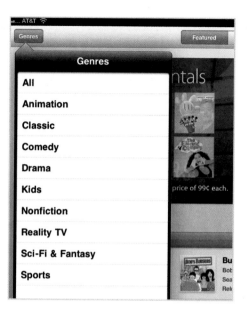

Sci-Fi & Fantasy, and Sports. If you're browsing movies, the Genres button includes some of the same categories as TV shows, and others like Thriller and Documentary. (Tap Genres again to hide the list.)

- **Featured**   Tap to view media that Apple thinks is noteworthy. The media listed here are handpicked by Apple. You'll see arrows that allow you to move left and right among the listings, and a button with a price for each one you see. There's also an option to "See All."

- **Top Charts**   Tap to see the most popular media for a specific category. This list will change often as the top sellers change.

- **Genius**   Tap to see if iTunes has any Genius suggestions for you. Genius will compile information about your preferences as you download media, and then offer recommendations for other media you might like (see Figure 6-2).

- **Search**   Tap to type keywords to locate specific media. You can search for artists, song titles, movie names, and more.

Browse and Buy Music

Tap the **Music** button to access music available from the iTunes Store. You'll see several panes, boxes, and lists, many of which were detailed previously.

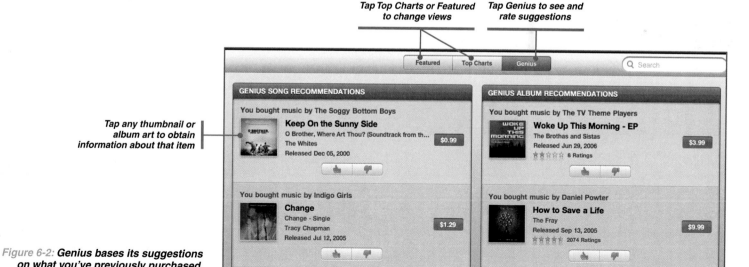

*Figure 6-2: **Genius bases its suggestions on what you've previously purchased.***

Tracy Chapman
New Beginning
Genre: Singer/Songwriter
Released: Dec 02, 1995
11 Songs
★★★★★ 60 Ratings

Artist Page ›
Tell a Friend ›

$9.99   👍 Like (128)   Post

Album Review

One might assume that the difference between Tracy Chapman's third album, which spent less than three months in the charts and failed to go gold after her first two albums had sold in the millions, and her fourth, which restored her to substantial commercial success, was th… **More ▼**

Tap to Preview

	Name	Time	Popularity	Price
1	Heaven's Here On Earth	5:23		$1.29
2	New Beginning	5:33		$1.29
3	Smoke and Ashes	6:39		$1.29
4	Cold Feet	5:40		$1.29

Figure 6-3: **Tapping an album cover offers more information about the album and artist.**

Tap to Preview

	Name	Time	Popularity	Price
1	Heaven's Here On Earth	5:23		BUY SONG
2	New Beginning	5:33		$1.29
3	Smoke and Ashes	6:39		$1.29

If you've never purchased music, you probably won't have any suggestions, but this is what Genius will look like after you do.

As you browse for music, you can tap the album artwork to open a window that details the media. From the information page that appears, shown in Figure 6-3, you'll find related information, such as a list of tracks on an album, user reviews and ratings, the option to view the Artist page or tell a friend (via e-mail), and more. To close the information window, tap anywhere outside of it.

Once you've found a song you like, you can purchase it. You'll see the price in a button beside the song, or you can purchase the entire album. Tap once to start the purchasing process. It will be an easy process, even the first time through, because you already set up an account with the store when you activated your iPad. You'll be prompted to input your password and to verify that you want to make the purchase, but it doesn't take more than a few seconds to get what you want.

To purchase a song:

1. Tap the price button beside any song or on its information page.
2. Tap **Buy Song**, **Buy Album**, or other relevant option.
3. Type your password.
4. Wait while the song downloads. If you want to watch the download process, tap the **Downloads** button on the bottom of the page.
5. You'll find the song, music video, or album in the iPod app.

Browse and Buy Movies

Your new iPad can play high-definition (HD) movies as well as standard-definition movies, which you can rent or buy from the iTunes Store. You

QUICKSTEPS

RENTING A MOVIE

You browse for, purchase (or rent), and download movies the same way you browsed for and purchased music earlier, and you have the same access to ratings and reviews. Use the tabs across the top of iTunes to locate the movie you want, and tap the appropriate icon to view the movie's information page. If a movie can be rented, you'll see two options. Tap **Buy** to purchase the movie, and tap **Rent** to rent it. When renting movies, note that rentals expire 24 hours after you begin viewing the media, and unwatched media can be retained for 30 days. It's important to note that not all movies can be rented, especially new releases.

1. Tap **iTunes** to open it.

2. Tap **Movies**.

3. Browse to the movie you want to rent.

4. Tap **View** to get more information about the movie.

5. Tap **Rent** if available.

6. If applicable, type your credentials to complete the purchase.

---

may never have purchased a movie from your iPad, but you browse and buy movies in the same manner as you browse and buy music.

1. Tap **iTunes** to open it.

2. Tap **Movies**.

3. If desired, tap **Featured**, **Top Charts**, or **Genius**.

4. If desired, tap **Genres** and tap any genre listed.

5. Tap **View** to get more information about the movie.

6. Tap **Preview**, if desired, to preview the movie.

7. Buy must be available to purchase the movie. It is possible only Rent is an option (in this case, see the QuickSteps "Renting a Movie"). Tap **Buy** to buy a movie.

Browse and Obtain Other Media

There are other types of media, as detailed earlier. Specifically, there are podcasts, audiobooks, and media from iTunes U (iTunes University).

OBTAIN PODCASTS

Podcasts are audio-only files that you download from iTunes and then listen to using the iPod app. Often, podcasts are the audio-only portion of a TV news show, independent interviews with authors or other notables, sermons from churches and synagogues, and similar media. Podcasts are so popular iTunes offers them in their own tab, shown in Figure 6-4.

Figure 6-4: *The Podcasts tab offers access to many genres of podcasts.*

OBTAIN TV SHOWS AND AUDIOBOOKS

TV shows are available from the TV Shows tab. There, you can rent or buy single episodes or purchase and watch entire seasons of your favorite shows. As with other tabs, you can tap the Genres button to filter the results.

There is also an Audiobooks tab. Audiobooks are digital books that someone, perhaps the author or an actor or actress, reads aloud and saves. You can purchase audiobooks in the same manner as you purchase music, movies, and other data. As with other tabs, you can tap the Categories button to filter the results.

USE iTUNES U

From the iTunes U tab, you can access audio and video files related to learning and higher education. Here you can obtain media to help you learn a new language or a new skill, or even listen to lectures given previously at Yale, Stanford, Berkeley, and other universities. You can browse museums virtually, explore information stored in the Library of Congress, and access various departments of education, among other things.

To obtain and listen to free media you find in iTunes U:

1. Tap **iTunes U** in iTunes.

2. Browse to locate the media you want to obtain. Look for the video icon by some offerings, denoting that the media is a video.

3. Tap the icon to access the Details page.

4. Tap **Free** and tap **Download**.

5. Tap the **Downloads** tab to follow the download process, if desired.

6. Once downloaded, close iTunes and open the iPod app. If the media is an audiobook or podcast, you can listen to it here. If you don't see it, look in the Videos app, under the appropriate tab. Figure 6-5 shows the Video app and the iTunes U tab.

Figure 6-5: **Use the Videos app to view videos you download from iTunes U, music videos, podcasts, and more.**

Get Apps from the App Store

The App Store is available from the App Store icon on the Home screen. Apps are programs you run on your iPad to perform specific tasks. You can get an app that helps you keep track of your workouts and weight loss, stay on top of breaking news, compare prices, or update your status on a social network, like Facebook, among other things.

Like iTunes, the App Store is configured with categories that make it easy to navigate. New, What's Hot, and Release Date run across the top. Featured, Genius, Top Charts, Categories, and Updates run across the bottom. You can also search from the Search window in the top-right corner. Figure 6-6 shows additional features of the App Store.

To use the App Store, you must be connected to the Internet. You'll also need an iTunes Store account, something you set up when you activated your iPad. To enter the store, simply tap the App Store icon on the Home screen. You can download and install all of the apps in the store, including apps designed for the iPhone and iPod touch. When searching for apps, try to stick to apps created specifically for the iPad, at least for now. You know these apps will take advantage of the iPad's larger screen and multitouch features, and will have been tested on an iPad. (Some apps created for the iPhone look distorted when you position them to take up the entire screen, even though they work as they should.) You can also sync apps you have already purchased for your iPhone or iPod touch using iTunes, if you want to try those apps on your iPad.

To browse apps by category:

1. Tap the **App Store** icon.
2. Tap any category to view the available apps. I suggest Top Charts and Top Free iPad Apps shown in Figure 6-7. You'll learn more about these in the next section.

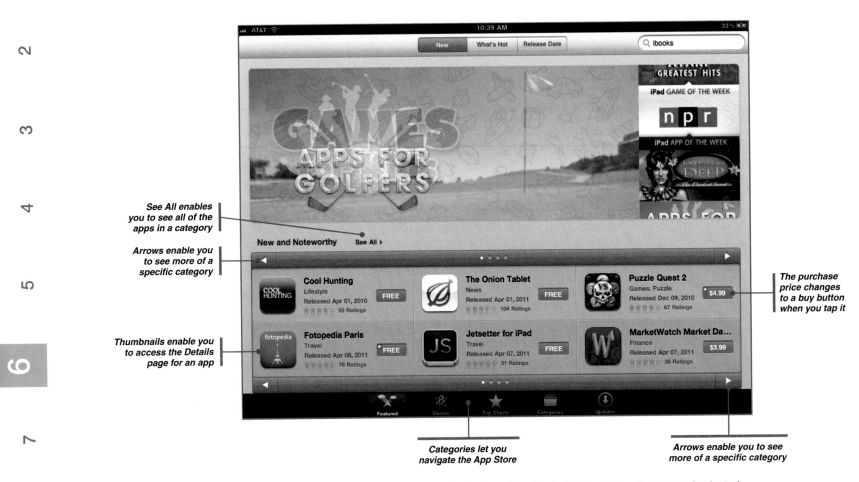

See All enables you to see all of the apps in a category

Arrows enable you to see more of a specific category

Thumbnails enable you to access the Details page for an app

The purchase price changes to a buy button when you tap it

Categories let you navigate the App Store

Arrows enable you to see more of a specific category

Figure 6-6: *The App Store offers various tabs for browsing; this is the New tab, with Featured selected.*

TIP

You could tap Free and then tap Install to get a free app, but it's best to read the reviews first.

Explore Top Paid and Top Free Apps

If you want to browse the most popular apps in the App Store, tap the **Featured** category at the bottom of the App Store interface, and tap **What's Hot** at the top. What's Hot shows what's "trending" at the moment. This doesn't mean the apps in this list have outsold all others or are more popular in the long term—it just means that at this moment, they're hot.

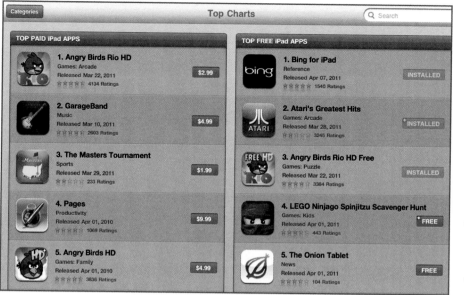

*Figure 6-7: **The Top Free section under Top Charts lets you experiment with apps without actually buying any; as you can see here, I've already installed some of these.***

There are free apps too, and the fact that they're free often makes them popular. There are free versions of games like Solitaire, free practical apps like calculators, and apps that let you play air guitar or a virtual piano. There are media apps from companies like Netflix, Time Warner, and ABC, and free newspapers, including *USA Today*.

To find popular and free apps for your iPad:

1. Tap the **App Store** icon.

2. Tap **Top Charts** at the bottom of the page.

3. In the right pane, scroll to browse the Top Free iPad apps.

Read Reviews of Apps

You should always read the reviews of applications before you purchase them. While an app may look good on an iPhone and have many excellent reviews, it may lose its luster on an iPad. In addition, app reviews can reveal bugs with an app, problems contacting the manufacturer, or information regarding the value of the app in comparison to its price. Finally, reviews can help uncover any problems with the app, such as it being too violent or sexual (like a game), or not including information required to make it useful (which is often the case with reference apps). The latter is more likely than the app being buggy; Apple keeps a pretty close eye on apps that don't work as they are designed to.

To find and read reviews for apps:

1. Tap the **App Store** icon.

2. Browse to an app.

3. Tap the app's icon.

4. Scroll down to the bottom of the Information page.

NOTE

The first time you use the App Store, you may be prompted to agree to terms of service. If so, tap **OK** to continue. Read and review the terms, and tap **Agree**. Note that you may have to tap **Agree** again. If prompted to "try your purchase again," start over with step 1. Agreeing to the terms of service is a one-time inconvenience, and you should not be prompted again unless the terms change.

Pages

Customer Ratings

Click to rate ☆ ☆ ☆ ☆ ☆

Average rating for the current version: ★★★★ 1069 Ratings

★★★★★	450
★★★★	299
★★★	154
★★	82
★	84

Customer Reviews

Write a Review ›

TIP

Visit Apple.com and tap **From The App Store**. From that page you can view a video about using iMovie and Garage Band, if you'd like more information.

TIP

Try the ABC Player, Facebook, Web MD, Netflix, iBooks, and other popular apps. They're popular for a reason.

NOTE

If you like an app and want to move it to another Home screen for easier access, tap and hold the icon for a second until all icons "wiggle," and then drag the app to its new location. Tap the **Home** key to apply the action.

5. Read any app review on the page; if there are more than will fit on one page, tap **More**.

6. Tap the **Back** button to return to the app's information page.

Explore iMovie and Garage Band

iMovie and Garage Band are two apps Apple is really promoting. Both iMovie and Garage Band are $4.99 as of this writing. If you want to make your own movies from video you shoot with your iPad, consider iMovie. If you want to create music using your iPad, consider Garage Band.

iMOVIE

iMovie helps you turn HD video you shoot from your iPad into professional-looking movies. To use it, you shoot the video with the camera, and then tap **iMovie**. You can select a theme, add music, insert photos, narrate the movie, and share your completed project with others in various ways. iMovie is compatible with the iPad 2, iPhone 4, and iPod touch (fourth generation).

GARAGE BAND

Garage Band offers virtual, digital musical instruments you can play and record, including guitars, basses, amps, drum sets, keyboards, and synthesizers. You "play" these devices and record what you create, and then you use the virtual music studio to blend them all together to mix them. This is an eight-track studio that enables you to create professional-sounding music tracks. As with iMovie, once you've completed a project, you can share the music you create in various ways, including e-mail and exporting to your iTunes library. Garage Band is compatible with the original iPad and the iPad 2.

Use an App

The first time you start an app, you'll probably see an introductory screen that either tells you how to use the app or offers a button for getting directions. After bypassing that, you may then see a menu screen that offers options for the app, like entering data, inputting a ZIP code or city, adding a player, or continuing where you left off the last time you used it. Because all apps are different,

SEARCHING FOR AND BUYING AN APP

To purchase and download an app:

1. Locate the app you want to purchase in the App Store.

2. Tap the app to go to its Information page, if desired.

3. Tap the price of the app. (Alternately, tap **Free** and tap **Install App.**)

4. If applicable, tap **Buy App.**

5. Type your iTunes password, if prompted. (If you've already made a purchase during this App Store session, you won't be asked for your password again.)

6. Watch the download process on your Home screen. Once the download is complete, tap the app to start it.

After you've used an app for a while, you may find that an update is available. You'll know when these updates are available because a number will appear on the App Store icon, and you'll see a number on the Updates tab of the App Store once it's opened. It's up to you whether or not to install updates. Always read the information offered about the update before installing it.

there's no way to be specific about what you'll see when you start an app and what you'll need to do to use it.

To start an app and use it:

1. Locate the icon for the app on the Home screen.

2. Tap the icon to start the app.

3. Read any introductory statements, and read any directions supplied.

4. Tap **Start**, **Play**, **Begin**, or another option. Once you've started an app, you may be prompted with instructions for play or use.

Get Books from the iBookstore

iBooks is a free app you obtain from the App Store that enables you to browse, download, and read digital books you obtain from the iBookstore contained within the app. It's an easy way to turn your iPad into a fully functional e-book reader. iBooks offers some innovative features, including touch screen control, support for color images, and embedded videos within some books. You can also create bookmarks, look up the definitions of words, change the font size, adjust the brightness of the screen, and more.

Install iBooks

iBooks isn't installed by default; you have to get it from the App Store. It's free, however; and since you have the option of reading free books too, you don't have to lay out any money to enjoy iBooks.

NOTE

You sync the books you purchase (to your computer) the same way you sync other media, using iTunes. Connect your iPad, select your iPad in the left pane, and click the **Books** tab. Then, opt to sync all books or configure what books to sync.

TIP

If you know the name of the book you want, type the title in the Search window.

TIP

Tap outside the information page to return to the store.

To install iBooks using your iPad:

1. Tap the **App Store** icon on the Home screen.
2. Tap **Featured**, **Top Charts**, **Genius**, or **Categories** at the bottom of the screen.
3. Tap inside the **Search** window, and type <u>iBooks</u>.
4. Tap **Free**, next to the iBooks icon.
5. Tap **Install**.

Browse the iBookstore

You must be connected to the Internet to browse the iBookstore. In iBooks, tap **Store** to enter. The interface is quite a bit like the iTunes Store and the App Store, and offers tabs, buttons, and categories. To browse books in the iBookstore:

1. Touch the **iBooks** app on the Home screen.
2. Tap **Store** in the top-left corner.

3. Tap **Featured** to view featured books.
4. Tap **Top Charts** to see a list of top paid and top free books.
5. Explore other options as desired, noting that the iBookstore is similar to the Apps Store and iTunes.
6. Tap **Library** to return to iBooks.

Explore the New York Times Bestseller List

One of the tabs in the iBookstore is NYTimes. The results are separated into fiction and nonfiction. You can scroll through the list by flicking up and down, and you can learn more about a book by tapping its icon. The resulting page offers information about the author, customer reviews, and a description of the book, among other things. Figure 6-8 shows an example of what you might see when you opt to learn more about a book on the list.

Figure 6-8: **The NYTimes tab offers an updated list of the most popular selling books at the moment.**

Sample a Book

From the information page of any book, you can tap **Get Sample** to read a small portion of it. Parts you can preview include (as applicable to the book):

- Table of contents
- Acknowledgments
- Forward
- A sample chapter or part of a chapter, or multiple chapters

To preview a book, click the **Get Sample** button inside the information page. A sample will download and will appear in your library. It will have a "Sample" banner across it.

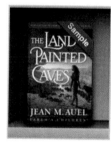

Read a Book

All of the books you've downloaded are on the virtual bookshelf. If you've downloaded any PDFs, they are there too, but you'll have to tap **Collections** and tap **PDFs** to get to them. (If you only see PDF files and not books, tap **Collections** and tap **Books**.) iBooks keeps books and PDFs separate to make them easier to find and manage.

To open and read a book:

1. Tap **iBooks**.
2. Tap any book on your bookshelf to read it.

UICKSTEPS

BUYING A BOOK

You can sample and then buy a book, or you can simply buy a book the same way you buy music or movies: by tapping the price and then the Buy button.

SAMPLE A BOOK

To get a sample of a book:

1. If you're in your library, tap **Store**.
2. Locate a book you want to sample.

Continued . . .

QUICKSTEPS

BUYING A BOOK *(Continued)*

3. Tap the book's icon to access the information page.

4. Tap **Get Sample**.

BUY A BOOK FROM A SAMPLE

To buy a book from a sample you've downloaded:

1. If you're in the store, tap **Library**.

2. Tap the sample book to open it.

3. Tap **Buy** on any page.

4. Input credentials if required.

BUY A BOOK FROM THE iBOOKSTORE

1. If you're in your library, tap **Store**.

2. Locate a book you want to buy.

3. Tap the price button.

4. Tap **Buy Book**.

TIP

To read a book while lying down, or to keep the iPad from switching views when you reposition yourself in a chair, enable the screen rotation lock. The screen rotation lock is located on the outside of your iPad above the volume buttons in portrait view or to the right of it in landscape view. If this lock mutes the iPad instead, change its behavior in Settings, under General; or double-tap the **Home** button, swipe the bottom bar that appears from left to right, and tap the **Screen Rotation** icon.

3. Hold the iPad in portrait or landscape orientation to view it as a single page or facing pages, respectively.

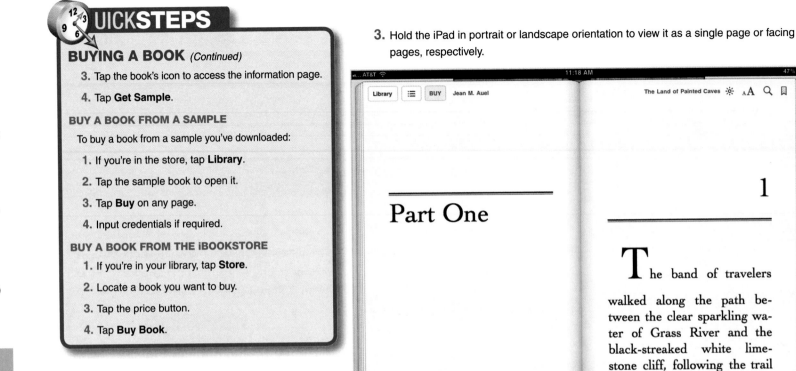

CHANGE THE FONT SIZE AND/OR BRIGHTNESS

You can adjust the text size and the font used in any book you get from the iBookstore. Everything you need is available on the top-right corner of iBooks. (If you don't see anything there, tap in the center of any page to show these controls.)

To increase or decrease the font size:

1. Tap the **Fonts** button.

2. To increase the font size, tap the **large A**. Tap again to increase the font size more.

3. To decrease the font size, tap the **small A**. Tap again to decrease the font size more.

NOTE

Your iPad will adjust the screen's brightness automatically. There's a sensor in the iPad that ascertains how much light is available and uses that information to make the adjustments. You can disable Auto-Brightness in Settings, under Brightness & Wallpaper, if you'd rather your iPad not do this automatically.

QUICKSTEPS

USING iBOOK CONTROLS

You can read and navigate iBooks in various ways. If you need to access controls and they aren't showing, tap in the center of the page.

READ A BOOK

- **Turn a page** Flick in the margin in the direction you wish to turn the page. Flick left to move forward in a book; flick right to move back.

- **Bookmark a page** Tap the bookmark icon in the top-right corner. Bookmarks is an option in Contents as well, detailed later, allowing you to access your bookmarks quickly.

- **Highlight a word or phrase** Tap and hold on the words you want to highlight. Drag from either end to highlight the text. Tap **Highlight**. (You can change the color of the highlight by tapping the highlighted text and selecting a new color from the list.)

- **Find the definition of a word** Tap and hold the word. Tap **Dictionary** from the options that appear.

Continued . . .

To change the font:

1. Tap the **Fonts** button.
2. Tap **Fonts**.
3. Tap a font in the list.

To change the brightness manually while reading a book in iBooks:

1. Tap the **Brightness** icon.
2. Drag to reposition the slider.

Manage Your Library

After you've used iBooks for a while, you may discover that you have too many books on your bookshelf and need to remove some. You may have so many books that you need to sort your books by their titles, authors, or by their category to find the book you want. You may even want to reorder the books on your bookshelf, placing the books you want to read in the order you plan to read them or create a new "collection" to hold them.

To sort books by their titles, authors, or categories:

1. Tap the **List** icon in the library. If you're in a book now, tap **Library** first.

2. At the bottom of the page, tap **Bookshelf**, **Titles**, **Authors**, or **Categories**. Categories is shown here.

Persuasion	Jane Austen
Pride and Prejudice	Jane Austen
Historical	
The Land of Painted Caves	Jean M. Auel
Mysteries & Thrillers	
The Cat Who Ate Danish Modern	Lilian Jackson Braun

Bookshelf   Titles   Authors   Categories

QUICKSTEPS

USING iBOOK CONTROLS *(Continued)*

FIND A SPECIFIC PART OF A BOOK

To access the controls, they must be showing. Tap in the center of any page to show them (or hide them).

- **Move to a specific page** Drag the slider to the desired page. Let go to jump to that page in the book.

Library	≣	BUY

- **Access the table of contents** Tap the **Contents** button.

- **Access a specific chapter** Tap the **Contents** button, and then tap the desired chapter in the table of contents. (Note the Resume button.)

- **Access your bookmarks** Tap the **Contents** button, tap the **Bookmarks** tab, and tap the bookmark.

Library	Resume	BUY	Jean M. Auel

#1 BESTSELLING AUTHOR OF *THE CLAN OF THE CAVE BEAR*

THE LAND OF PAINTED CAVES

The Land of Painted Caves

TABLE OF CONTENTS	BOOKMARKS

Other Books by This Author	2
Title Page	3
Copyright	4
Dedication	7
Acknowledgments	8
Map	33
Part One	38
Chapter 1	39

To reposition the books on your bookshelf:

1. Tap the **Thumbnail** icon. The Thumbnail icon is to the left of the Edit button and consists of four small squares.

2. Tap **Edit**.

3. Drag and drop any book to a new position on the bookshelf.

4. Click the **Done** button when finished.

To delete a book:

1. In any view, tap **Edit**.

2. Tap **Delete** and tap **Delete** again to verify.

3. Repeat as desired and then click **Done**.

The library offers a button called Collections. Tap it to see the two available collections: Books and PDFs. The default view is Books, but if you download and need to access PDFs, you'll find them in the PDF collection. You can also create your own "collection." Once created, you can move books there to organize them.

1. In Library view, tap **Collections**.

2. Tap **New**.

3. Type the name for the new collection. I have two here, Cooking and Cats, and am adding Travel.

4. Tap **Done**.

5. Repeat as desired.

6. Tap outside the collections window when complete.

Store	Collections

| Books |
| PDFs | ✓ |
| Cooking |
| Cats |
| Travel |

| New | Done |

NOTE

Deleted books remain in your iTunes library on your computer provided you've previously opted to sync books and have actually synced them.

To move a book into a collection you've created:

1. In Library view, tap **Edit**.

2. Tap a book to select it.

3. Tap **Move**.

4. Tap the collection you want to move the book to.

5. Note the new view with the book moved. Tap **Collections** to return to any other collection.

Chapter 7

Exploring More On-board Apps

You've been exploring apps throughout this book and have become familiar with many of them. Now it's time to explore some additional apps included with your iPad, specifically YouTube, Maps, and the Game Center. Once you know how to use these three apps, you can likely deduce easily how to use others.

Have Fun with YouTube

The YouTube app enables you to easily browse YouTube videos right from your iPad. If you have a YouTube account (it's free), you can sign in and access videos you've uploaded yourself from your computer or from your iPad, rate and comment on videos, view your subscriptions, and more. You can even e-mail a link to a video to someone to share it.

If you aren't quite sure what YouTube is, in a few words it's a video-sharing website where users can upload and share videos they take or movies they

QUICKSTEPS

PLAYING YOUTUBE VIDEOS

Browse the videos using the category buttons outlined here, or search for a specific video with Search. Tap a video to play it. The controls you'll use once a video is playing will look like controls you've seen in other apps, specifically the apps for the iPod detailed in Chapter 5. As detailed there, you can play, pause, fast-forward, and rewind easily.

SWITCH BETWEEN MODES

Depending on several factors, your video may open in full-screen mode or it may only take up a small portion of the screen. You can easily switch between modes by pinching your fingers apart or together.

CONTROL PLAYBACK IN FULL-SCREEN MODE

Tap while in full-screen mode to access the available controls. They include Bookmark, Skip Back (to previous video), Play/Pause, and Skip Forward (to the next video). On the right is the option to change the view from full screen to its smaller counterpart. You can also access the hi-speed scrubbing slider at the top of the page to quickly locate a specific part of a video (not shown).

CONTROL PLAYBACK IN HALF-SCREEN MODE

Tap the video while in the half-screen mode to access the available controls. These are introduced in Figure 7-1. Remember, you can move from half-screen to full-screen mode by pinching.

NOTE

There's a Search window in the YouTube interface, and it works just like any Search window in any other iPad app. Just tap it to type in keywords for videos you'd like to see.

create. Companies and artists also use YouTube to share clips of movies they produce, commercials they create for their products, TV show teasers, and music videos. Most of the video on YouTube is created and uploaded by individuals, and runs the gamut from funny to serious to downright filthy.

The YouTube app offers several different views. Figure 7-1 shows the Most Viewed option selected across the bottom, with Related, More From, and Comments on the right, and the selected video available on the left. When you tap the video, the controls appear, also shown.

Search YouTube Videos

You have to be connected to the Internet to access YouTube. Because YouTube videos require that quite a bit of data be transferred, if you have a limited data plan, be careful how much time you spend here. Alternately, you could connect to a free Wi-Fi network before continuing. That said, as with other apps, there are familiar buttons across the bottom:

- **Featured** These are apps that are featured by YouTube because they're unique, meaningful, funny, or exhibit some other reason for featured status.

- **Top Rated** When viewers watch videos, they also often rate them. The videos in this category are the highest-rated videos of the day, week, and all time.

- **Most Viewed** YouTube keeps track of how often viewers watch a video, and the videos in this category have more views than the others.

- **Favorites** The videos here are ones you bookmark as videos you like. (The bookmark icon is the same icon you have access to in Safari.) You can then access your favorite videos anytime you want to watch them again or show them to a friend.

- **Subscriptions** If you like a particular YouTube user, you can subscribe to them. You can then view all videos posted by that person easily, as well as any new videos they post.

- **My Videos** If you've uploaded any of your own video to YouTube, you'll have easy access to it here. You can also see how many people have viewed your video and read any comments that have been posted.

- **History** The videos you've viewed on YouTube are listed here. This offers an easy way to access a video again, should you desire.

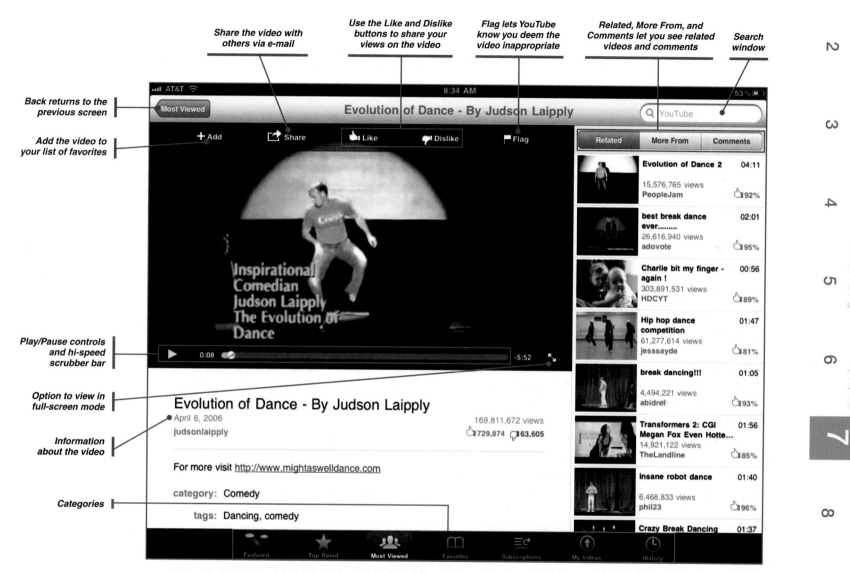

Back returns to the previous screen

Add the video to your list of favorites

Share the video with others via e-mail

Use the Like and Dislike buttons to share your views on the video

Flag lets YouTube know you deem the video inappropriate

Related, More From, and Comments let you see related videos and comments

Search window

Play/Pause controls and hi-speed scrubber bar

Option to view in full-screen mode

Information about the video

Categories

Figure 7-1: *The YouTube app offers various features and navigational tools.*

Rate and Comment on Videos

You have to create a YouTube account and sign in to it to rate a video or leave a comment. This simply consists of navigating to www.youtube.com, tapping **Sign In**, and then signing up for a free account.

To rate and comment on YouTube videos:

1. Locate a video you want to comment on or rate.
2. Tap the video screen while in the smaller mode, and tap **Like** or **Dislike**.
3. When prompted, as shown in Figure 7-2, type your YouTube username and password. Tap **Sign In**.
4. Tap **Comments** in the right pane to write your own comments. Tap in the **Add A Comment** window, and begin typing. Tap **Send** (on the keyboard) when finished.
5. You can also flag a video if you find it offensive. Tap **Flag** to get started.

Figure 7-2: **You'll be prompted to sign in the first time you try to like or dislike a video.**

Share a YouTube Video

You can tap **Share**, shown earlier in Figure 7-1, to e-mail a link to a video to someone you think would enjoy it. Of course, you'll need to have the Mail app set up (see Chapter 3), and you'll need the e-mail address of the person you'd

UPLOADING YOUR OWN VIDEO

You can take video with your iPad's video camera and upload it to YouTube, provided you have a YouTube account and the video is smaller than 2GB and is of an acceptable file format. You learned about the Photos app and the Camera app in Chapter 4. If you need to, refer to that chapter to acquire some video. Alternately, you can sync video files from your computer using iTunes. Once your video is saved, you can upload it to YouTube.

To upload video from your iPad to YouTube:

1. Tap the **Photos** app.
2. Locate the video and tap it.
3. Tap the **Share** button, and tap **Send To YouTube**. (Sign in if required.)

Continued . . .

UPLOADING YOUR OWN VIDEO
(Continued)

4. Type a title and description, choose a quality setting, include tags, choose a category, and choose who can view the video (**Public** or **Unlisted**).

Publish Video

Cancel | Publish

My first video

Uploading my first video to YouTube!

Standard Definition (~301KB) ✓

HD (~901KB)

Tags

Category — Comedy

Public
Anyone can search for and view

Unlisted
Anyone with a link can view

Private
Only specific YouTube users can view ✓

5. Tap **Publish**.

6. When prompted, tap **View On YouTube**, **Tell A Friend**, or **Close**.

like to send the link to, but you probably already have all of that. When your e-mail is received, it'll look something like this to the recipient.

From: (Joli Ballew)

Charlie bit my finger - again !
April 13, 2011 8:49 AM ● Mark as Unread

Check out this video on YouTube:

http://www.youtube.com/watch?v=_OBlgSz8sSM&feature=youtube_gdata_player

Sent from my iPad

Navigate with Maps

The Maps app offers directions to and from almost anywhere, and the ability to share those directions easily with others. You can incorporate Maps with Google's Street View (when available) to view a picture of your destination, and you can access driving routes, walking routes, and public transportation routes easily. You can search for points of interest, landmarks, businesses, restaurants, or even a specific intersection. You can easily find your present location, and if a location isn't marked on a map, such as a friend's house or park, you can mark it yourself and save it as a bookmark. Figure 7-3 shows the Maps interface.

Find Your Present Location

The best way to explore the Maps app is to first find your current location and then tap the various options for views to see how they look. Because you're probably familiar with your surroundings, you can easily recognize what's around you. Once the iPad knows your current location, you can easily browse nearby streets, businesses, and even the current traffic, if available. To find your present location, tap the **Location** button.

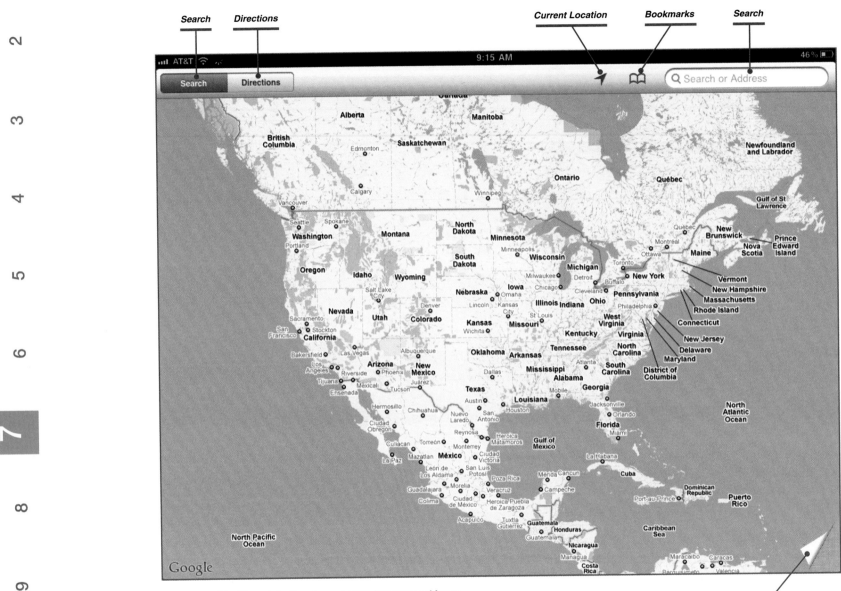

Search Directions   Current Location   Bookmarks   Search

Figure 7-3: **The Maps interface has various buttons and icons.**

Page Turner/Dog Ear

NOTE

If prompted, let Maps access your current location with location services.

QUICK**FACTS**

UNDERSTANDING THE MAPS INTERFACE

You open the Maps app the same way you open any app: by tapping it once. There are several interface features to explore, and they are arranged familiarly with buttons and tabs.

THE TOOLBAR

The toolbar consists of the following options:

- **Search** Type information to view something on the map, including landmarks, airports, and other recognizable data.

- **Directions** Access two windows you can fill in to get directions from one place to another. You can get directions from your present location to a new location or using any two addresses.

- **Current location** Show your present location on a map. A blue dot appears to denote where you are.

- **Bookmarks** Tap the **Bookmarks** icon to see the bookmarks you've previously saved and tap any bookmark listed there to show its location on a map.

Continued . . .

With your present location available:

1. Tap the blue dot and then the blue i to learn more about your location, including the address, the option to share your location with others, create a bookmark, and even view a picture, if available.

2. If a thumbnail of your current location is available, tap it. Tap the screen and tap **Done** to return to Maps.

3. Touch the bottom-right corner of the map on the dog ear. (See the QuickFacts "Understanding the Maps Interface" for more explanation.)

4. Touch any view option to see that view on the map.

5. Repeat to explore all views.

UNDERSTANDING THE MAPS INTERFACE

(Continued)

THE DOG EAR

The dog ear feature lets you see "underneath" the Maps interface. Here, you'll find options to change the view and access additional options:

- **Classic**   To view the map with street names, parks, and water included.

- **Satellite**   To view the location as it appears from the sky.

- **Hybrid**   To view a map in Classic and Satellite view, together.

- **Terrain**   To view the map with terrain features, such as elevation.

- **Traffic**   To show traffic conditions, if available. Colors that denote traffic are red, yellow, and green.

- **Drop Pin**   To drop a pin anywhere on a map to make a note of it.

Map	
Classic	✓
Satellite	
Hybrid	
Terrain	

Overlays	
Traffic	OFF
Drop Pin	

Terms of Use...

6. In any view, use your finger to scroll through the map.

7. While in any map and in any view, try out these navigational techniques:

   - Pinch your fingers toward each other to zoom out of a map.

   - Pull your fingers outward to zoom in on an area on a map.

   - Tap twice to zoom in. (Pinch to zoom back out.)

   - Reposition the iPad from landscape to portrait view and back by turning the iPad 90 degrees left or right.

   - Tap and drag across the screen to see more of the map.

Get Directions

You can get directions in a number of ways. You can type in any address to obtain driving directions to the address from your present location, and scroll through maps digitally to view the terrain or route. If you need directions from one place to another but one of those places is not your current address, you can type in two addresses. This enables you to obtain directions from a starting point to an end point; from anywhere to anywhere.

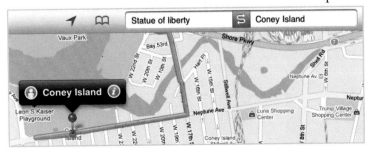

To find an address and get directions to it:

1. In Maps, tap **Directions**.

2. Tap the **Location** icon to make sure Maps can pinpoint where you are.

3. To start from an address other than your current location, tap in that window, and type a new address.

4. Tap in the second window to type the ending address.

NOTE

When obtaining directions, you can type something other than an address. You can search for a business name, landmark, or other entity.

5. Tap **Search** on the keyboard.

6. At the bottom of the page, tap the driving icon. It looks like a car. (You can also tap the bus icon or the walking icon.)

7. Click **Start** and then advance through the directions using the arrow buttons.

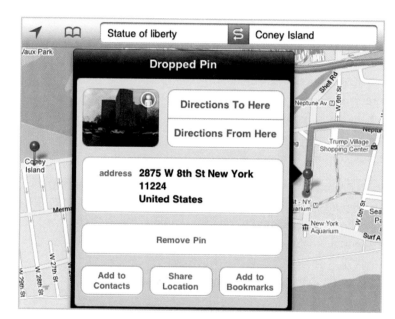

Mark a Location

When you search for a restaurant or business, Maps sets down a pin in its location. You touch the pin to get more information about it, including directions to it. Not all locations have pins, however. A brand-new restaurant won't, and neither will your home. You can add your own pins simply by tapping and holding an area of the screen.

To mark a location and save it as a bookmark:

1. Find the location on a map.

2. Tap and hold to drop a pin.

3. Tap the **i** to open the information page.

4. To name the location and save it, tap **Add To Bookmarks**, and name the bookmark as desired.

5. Tap **Save**.

Explore Street View

Street View is a view available via Google Maps that allows you to view pictures of a location or your destination. This feature provides 360-degree views of many locations across the world. You can access these images from the information window that appears in the pin associated with a location. When

TIP

If you'd like to invite others to meet you at a location, you can click **Share Location**, which is available on any information page. Tap it, and a new e-mail will open, where you can complete the invitation.

American Airlines Center

Directions To Here

Directions From Here

phone **+1 (214) 221-8326**

home page **http://www.americanairline...**

address **2500 Victory Ave
Dallas Texas
United States**

Add to
Contacts

Share
Location

Add to
Bookmarks

©2010 Google

TIP

To hide an information window, tap outside of it. To show
it again, tap the pin on the map.

Street View is available, you'll see a thumbnail in the information window. To
see the picture in full-screen view, tap it.

While in full-screen mode you can drag your finger across the
screen to see what's to the left and right of the location, or even
what's across the street. When you're finished exploring, tap the
small icon in the bottom-right corner to return to Maps.

Use the Game Center

The Game Center offers access to an online gaming network. Basically, it's an
Apple-designed alternative to third-party matchmaking, leaderboard, and
achievement tracking services, which will only mean something to you if you're
a big fan of gaming! In layman's terms, the Game Center's purpose is to match
up users who choose to play games against each other online, or to enable
players to invite people they know or have previously met to play a game, and
to let those players keep track of their scores and achievements.

You can also use the Game Center to download games, review the status of the
gaming friends you make, and see friend requests, among other things. You'll
have to sign in with your Apple ID to get started, and download games you
want to play. After that, you're ready to compete!

Sign In to the Game Center

Tap the **Game Center** icon, and input your Apple ID and password to get
started. Tap **Sign In**. If you're prompted to create an account, do so. This will
include choosing your country, inputting your date of birth, agreeing to some
terms of service, creating a secret word or question, inputting the answer,
creating a nickname, and deciding if you'd like to allow game invitations
and other communications (you'll need to allow game invitations to play
multiplayer online games). Once you've done all that, you're ready to play
(see Figure 7-4)!

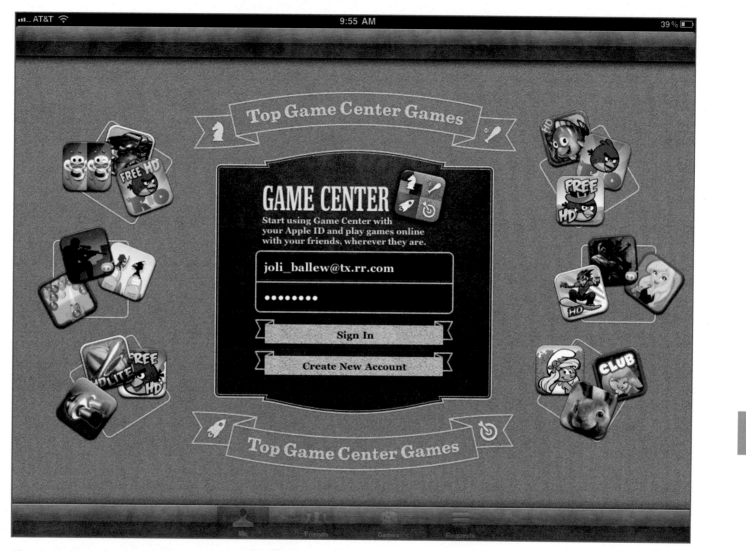

Figure 7-4: *Open the Game Center and sign in to get started.*

Understand the Interface

You'll notice, after signing in, that there are four options across the bottom of the Game Center interface. They include:

- **Me** This view shows your name, nickname, friends, games, achievements, and other information. You can type your status. You can also tap any game's icon here to go the App store to get the game.

- **Friends** This view shows your friends, their status, and other information, and offers a way to add more friends.

- **Games** This view offers access to games you've recently played, your achievements, leaderboards, and a place to share news about a game with friends.

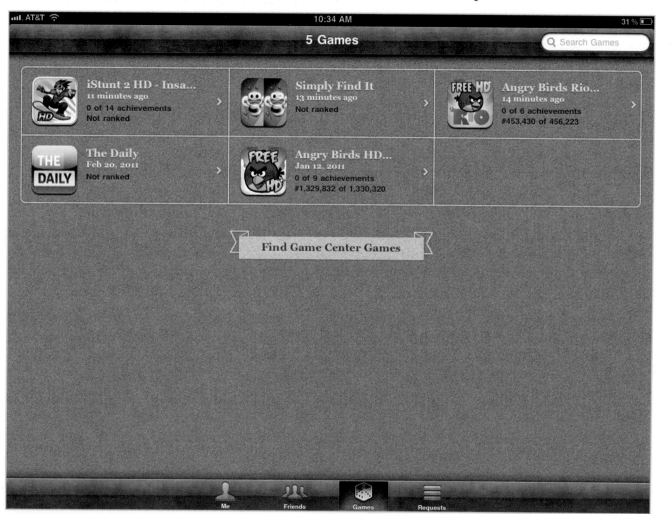

- **Requests** This view offers information about friend requests and gives you the option to ignore, accept, or report a problem.

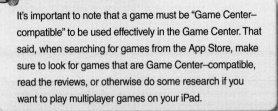

Get and Play a Game

There are several ways to find games, but one of the easiest is to open the Game Center, tap **Games**, and tap **Find Game Center Games**. This will take you to the App Store where you can search for and download games as desired. Alternately, you can tap the **Me** button, and tap an icon for a game you recognize to go directly to that page in the App Store. Once you've downloaded a game, tap it on the appropriate iPad screen to start it, and work through any setup pages. You may see, during setup, that a game is Game Center–compatible.

The game you're playing also uses Game Center.

Most Game Center–compatible games offer multiplayer modes, which bring up a Game Center matchmaking screen. This enables you to invite friends to play games with you. If you don't have enough friends to play against in a given game, the Game Center includes Auto-Match, which will match you up against another player who is also interested in playing right now. When all players are ready, you can start playing together.

As an example, in Pool Bar, Online Hustle, the first screen asks if you'd like to incorporate the Game Center, and then offers the option to play the game online. To be automatically matched with another player, you can tap **Play**, or you can opt to invite a friend (see Figure 7-5.)

Once you've been matched up, you're ready to play.

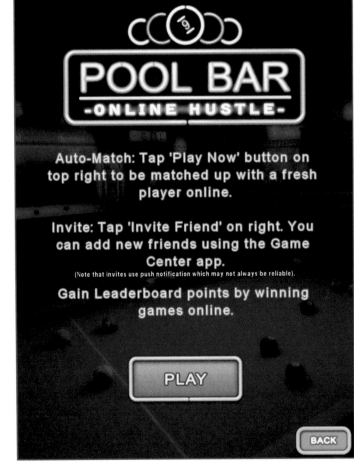

Figure 7-5: **Some games offer the ability to be matched with other players online.**

Chapter 8
Managing Contacts and Calendars

In this chapter you'll learn about two of the more practical apps available on your iPad: Contacts and Calendar. If you've ever used an e-mail program, cell phone, instant messaging program, or even an old-fashioned Rolodex, you're familiar with contacts. A contact is a person or company you, well, contact, via e-mail, phone, text message, instant message, letter, fax, or other medium. You're probably equally versed with calendars, too. Even if you've never used a digital calendar, you'll have no trouble adapting to the Calendar app on the iPad.

Communicate with and Manage Contacts

Your iPad comes with a Contacts app that allows you to keep digital contacts. When you add a contact manually, you can input the usual information: e-mail

Let the Calendar app send you a reminder a day or two before a person's birthday or your anniversary, so you don't forget it!

address, phone number, street address, ZIP code, and the like, but you can also add personal information, such as birthdays, anniversaries, and even children's names. You also can add a picture. Beyond adding the information, you can access contact information from various other apps, like Mail and Calendar. Figure 8-1 shows the Contacts app. Tap the Contacts app to open it.

Search for a contact by name

Group your contacts

View an alphabetical list of contacts

Groups

Collected Contacts

Q Search

12:33 PM   27%

..... AT&T

A B C D E F G H I J K L M N O P Q R S T U V W X Y Z #

No Contacts

Add A Contact

+

Figure 8-1: *The Contacts app has several interface features.*

NOTE

You'll learn how to sync both contacts and calendar data in Chapter 10.

Add a Contact

You may or may not have any contacts in the Contacts app. You will have contacts if you've synced them from your computer, synced them from the cloud, or manually added them from Mail. If you've yet to take any of these steps, you can manually add a contact to get started.

Create a Contact

You can add various types of information to a contact, including a picture. Figure 8-2 shows a Contact card with the keyboard hidden to show a few of the items you can add.

ADD BASIC INFORMATION

To add basic contact information:

1. Open the Contacts app.

2. Tap the plus sign (+).

3. Fill in basic information, shown in Figure 8-2, including but not limited to:

  a. First and last name

  b. Phone number

  c. E-mail address

  d. Street address

  e. City, state, and ZIP code

4. Leave the Contact card open.

ADD OTHER INFORMATION

To add other information:

1. Scroll down to the bottom of the Contact card, and tap the green plus sign next to "add field." Note all the fields you can add, including but not limited to:

  a. Prefix

  b. Phonetic First Name

  c. Phonetic Last name

Tap to choose a photo stored on your iPad or take a photo with the camera

Basic information, including first and last name, phone, and e-mail, are important to add

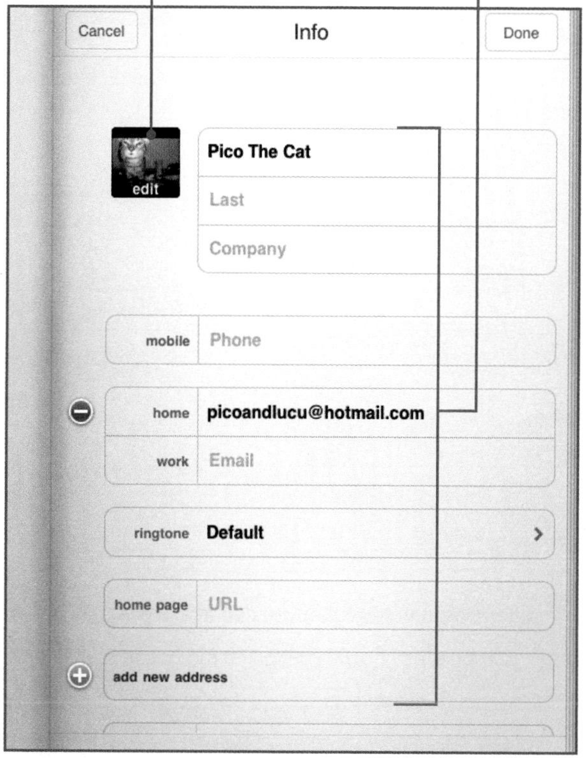

Cancel	Info	Done

Pico The Cat

Last

Company

mobile   Phone

home   picoandlucu@hotmail.com

work   Email

ringtone   **Default**

home page   URL

add new address

Figure 8-2: *When you add a contact, you can include as little or as much information as you like.*

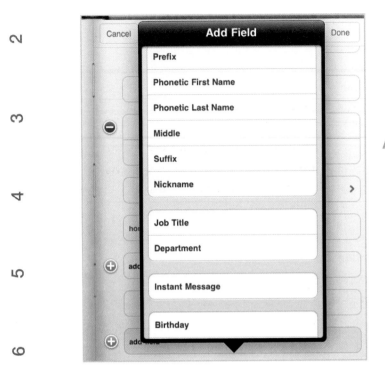

d. Nickname

e. Job Title

f. Birthday

2. Depending on the option you chose in step 1, you'll have the option to input information regarding that field.

3. Leave the Contact card open.

ADD A PICTURE

To add a picture for a contact:

1. With a Contact card open, tap **Add Photo** in the top-left corner. (We've tapped **Edit** here because we already have a photo configured.)

2. Tap **Take Photo** or **Choose Photo**.

3. Either tap the folder that contains the picture you want to add (and tap the picture you decide to use) or take a picture with the camera.

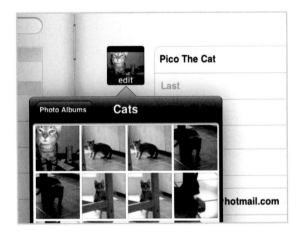

TIP

When selecting a picture or taking one, try to use a head shot. It'll be easier to see on the Contact card.

4. If desired, drag to move and scale the picture. Note that you can also pinch to resize it.

5. Tap **Use**; tap **Done**. The image will appear as shown, giving you the option to edit it if desired.

Locate a Contact

The Contacts app is one of the simpler apps to use. It looks like the physical address book you're probably already familiar with, and includes alphabetical

GETTING A MAP TO A CONTACT'S ADDRESS

You can get a map to a contact's home or place of business quickly, provided you've previously input that information in the Contact card. To bring up a map:

1. Open the Contacts app.

2. Use any method desired to locate the contact.

3. Touch the contact to open their Contact card.

4. Touch the address.

5. Maps will open, and you can obtain the desired directions.

tabs to let you access a page quickly. You can scroll through the contacts to locate the one you want.

1. Position the iPad in landscape view.

2. Tap **Contacts** to open the app.

3. In the All Contacts list, flick up or down to scroll through the list; alternately, tap any letter on the left side to go to that section of the Contacts list.

As your Contacts list grows, tapping a letter in the left margin and/or scrolling may not be the best way to locate the contact you want. If this happens, you can search for any contact in the Search window. You can use this window to type in a part of your contact's name and view the results in a list.

To search for a contact:

1. In the Contacts app, locate the Search window.

2. Tap inside the **Search** window to bring up the virtual keyboard.

3. Type the first few letters of the name of the contact you'd like to find.

4. Tap the contact to view the Contact card.

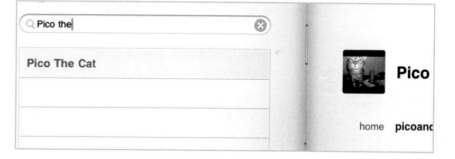

E-mail a Contact

The main reason you add contacts on your iPad is almost always to make it easier to e-mail them. You may add yourself as a contact, too, so that you can easily share your contact information with others, and you may add a contact just so you'll have easy access to a map to their home, but for the most part, contacts you add are for e-mailing. In Mail, most of the time you only need to type a few letters of the contact's name and the information for that contact appears wherever it's needed (like the To line in an e-mail).

You have a couple of options for sending e-mail to a contact. You can open the Contact card for a person you'd like to e-mail in Contacts, and click their e-mail address to open a new message in Mail; or you can open the Mail app and start a new e-mail, and type part of the contact's name in the To line to add them.

To send an e-mail to a contact from the Contacts app:

1. Open Contacts and locate the contact you want to e-mail.

2. Tap their name to open their Contact card.

3. Tap their e-mail address to have Mail open automatically and insert the e-mail address in the To line.

TIP

If you receive an e-mail from someone you do not yet have in your Contacts list, tap the sender in the From line, and tap **Create New Contact**. Alternately, you can tap **Add To Existing Contact**.

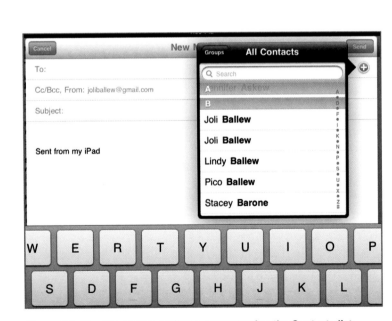

Figure 8-3: **You can send e-mail to a contact using the Contacts list.**

To send an e-mail from the Mail app:

1. Tap **Mail** to open it.

2. Tap the **Compose** button.

3. Tap the plus sign to locate a contact you want to add, or type the first letter of their first or last name to select them from another list that appears (see Figure 8-3).

Organize with Calendar

The Calendar app is available from the Home screen; tap it once to open it. If you haven't already synced calendar events through iTunes, you'll only see an empty calendar, shown in Figure 8-4. Note the various view options; this is Month view.

Tap to show a list of any additional calendars you've configured or subscribed to

Tap to change the view

Tap to search for something in Calendar

Figure 8-4: **The Calendar offers various views and features to help you get and stay organized.**

Tap to locate today on the calendar

Tap any month to go there quickly

Tap to add an event

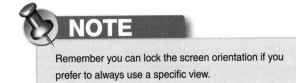

To open the Calendar and explore the interface:

1. Tap the **Calendar** app on the Home screen.

2. At the top of the Calendar app, tap **Day**, **Week**, **Month**, or **List**.

3. Turn the iPad 90 degrees to rotate from landscape view to portrait view.

Create a Calendar Entry

The best way to integrate the Calendar app with your iPad is to input some data. Think about all of the things you could input. To get started, you could create events for a few birthdays or an anniversary, or anything you do every week or every month, such as an exercise class or dinner date. During the event creation process, you can also opt to add reminders. These reminders are essential if you don't plan to look at the Calendar app every day. When you create a reminder, you'll get a pop-up message on your iPad. You'll still have to look at your iPad to get the reminder, however. The Add Event window is shown in Figure 8-5.

To add an event to the calendar and add alerts and reminders:

1. Open the **Calendar** app.

2. Tap the plus sign.

3. Type the desired information:

    a. **Title**   Tap to add a descriptive title for the event. If you're adding a birthday, for instance, type <u>Cosmo's Birthday</u>.

    b. **Location**   Tap to add a location, if applicable.

    c. **Start and End Times** (or all-day event)   Tap to configure the start and end times, or to create an all-day event. Click **Done** after entering the desired information. Note that when you tap this option, a new window appears.

    d. **Repeat**   Tap to set the event to repeat. Choose from None, Every Day, Every Week, Every 2 Weeks, Every Month, or Every Year. Click **Done** when finished. Use the End Repeat setting to determine when an event no longer needs to repeat.

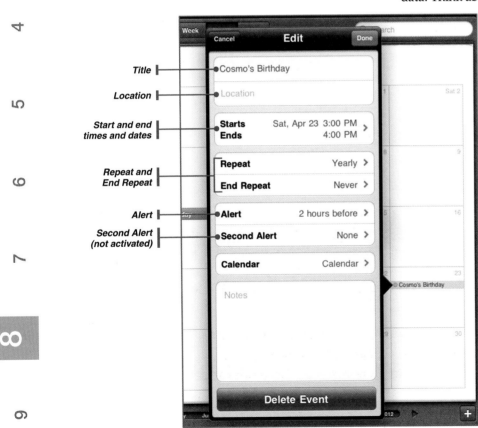

Figure 8-5: The Add Event window offers areas to input and configure information, dates, and times for the event.

e. **Alert** Tap **Alert** to set an alert. Choose from None, 5 Minutes Before, 15 Minutes Before, 30 Minutes Before, 1 Hour Before, 2 Hours Before, 1 Day Before, 2 Days Before, or On Date Of Event. Tap **Done** when finished.

f. **Calendar** Tap **Calendar** to choose a calendar *if more than one exists.* What you see here will differ based on the calendars you have access to, and this option won't appear if you only have one calendar configured. When you add an event to a specific calendar, it will appear on that calendar. Click **Done** when finished.

g. **Notes** Tap to type notes regarding the event.

4. After all the information is added, tap **Done**.

5. Notice the new event on the calendar. Tap the event and tap **Edit** to edit the event, if desired.

NOTE

You can tap any entry and tap **Edit** to access any event's properties.

Dinner with Dad
Applebee's   5 PM to 6 PM   Edit
alert   1 hour before

Dinner with Dad

Create a Second Calendar

You can configure multiple calendars to manage your different responsibilities. You can create a calendar just for work, one for athletic endeavors, one for the hours you're responsible for taking care of an aging parent, and another to hold your children's sports schedules. Each calendar you create stands alone. Each calendar has events listed in its own color, and each calendar can be viewed with any other calendar when needed.

Creating a second or third calendar isn't something you do on your iPad. You create additional calendars in the calendar application you use on your computer. Make sure to create these calendars on the computer you've been using to sync your iPad. Once you've created the desired calendars, you sync them using iTunes.

1. Connect your iPad to your computer.

2. Select your iPad in the left pane of iTunes.

TIP

Apple provides a number of free calendars if you'd like to try them out, including calendars for national holidays and sports events.

QUICKSTEPS

SUBSCRIBING TO A THIRD-PARTY CALENDAR

To subscribe to a calendar available from Apple:

1. Tap **Safari** and navigate to www.icalshare.com.
2. Note the calendar categories.
3. Locate a calendar you'd like to include, and tap to select it.
4. Tap **Subscribe To Calendar**.

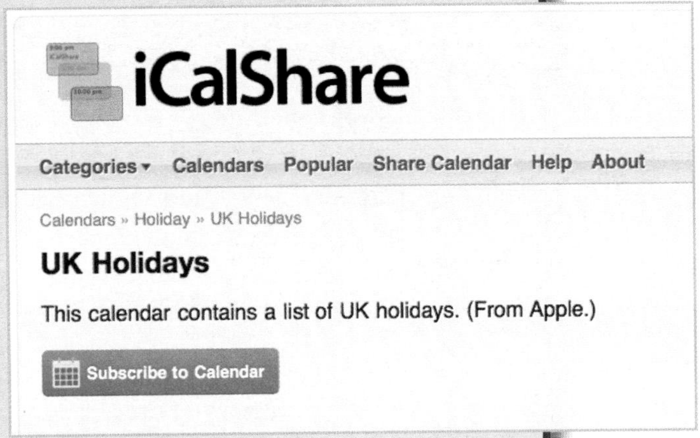

iCalShare
Categories
Calendars
Popular
Share Calendar
Help
About
Calendars » Holiday » UK Holidays
UK Holidays
This calendar contains a list of UK holidays. (From Apple.)
Subscribe to Calendar

5. Tap **Subscribe**. Tap **Done**.
6. Open the Calendar app.
7. Tap **Calendars**.

Continued . . .

3. Click the **Info** tab.
4. Select **Sync Calendars With**, and select the calendar program you currently use.
5. Opt to sync all calendars or only specific calendars, and make the required selections (see Figure 8-6).
6. Once the sync is complete, on your iPad:
   a. Tap **Calendar**.
   b. Tap **Calendars** in the top-left corner.
   c. If necessary, tap **Show All Calendars**.
   d. Note the new calendars.

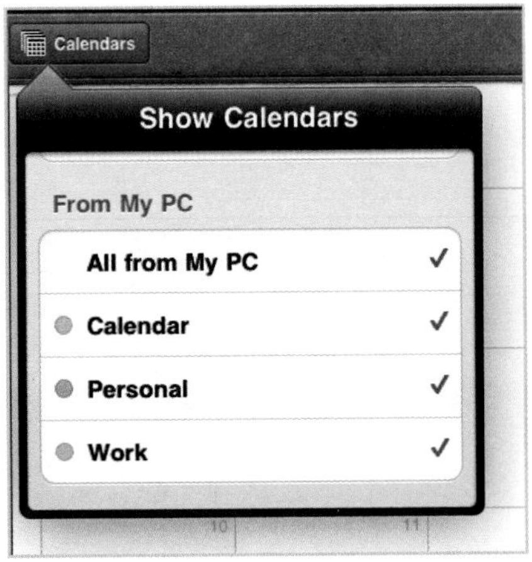

Calendars
Show Calendars
From My PC
All from My PC
Calendar
Personal
Work

You can now work with the additional calendars just as you worked with a single one. The only exception is that you should know how to hide or show calendars as needed.

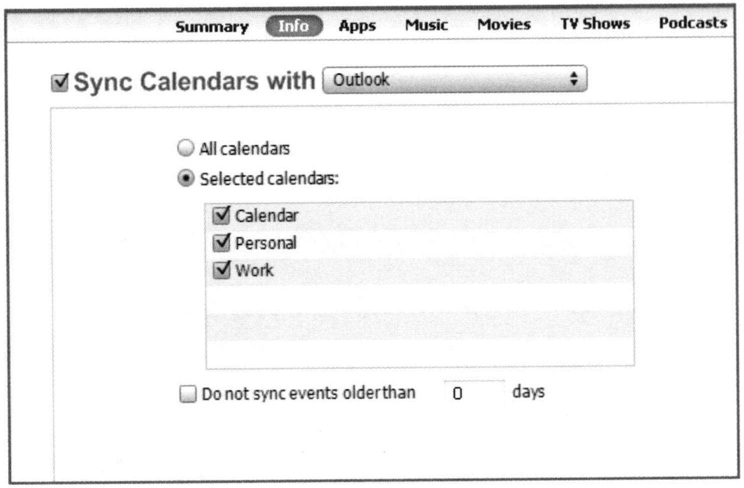

Summary
Info
Apps
Music
Movies
TV Shows
Podcasts
Sync Calendars with
Outlook
All calendars
Selected calendars:
Calendar
Personal
Work
Do not sync events older than
0
days

Figure 8-6: ***Select the calendars you want to sync.***

QUICKSTEPS

SUBSCRIBING TO A THIRD-PARTY CALENDAR *(Continued)*

8. Tap the new calendar to display it.

Show Calendars

Show All Calendars

From My PC

All from My PC

● **Calendar** ✓

● **Personal** ✓

● **Work**

Subscribed

● **UK Holidays** ✓
   Subscribed

9. Tap outside the Calendar options window to close it, and note the new calendar entries.

20	21	22	23
	● Queen's Birthday	● Good Friday	● St. George's Day
		● Dinner with Dad	● Cosmo's Birthday

Show Multiple Calendars

To view a single calendar and show multiple calendars at once:

1. In the Calendar app, tap **Calendars**.

2. Tap any calendar to show or hide it. If it has a check mark by it, the calendar will be displayed; if not, it will be hidden.

Subscribe to a Calendar

You can subscribe to compatible calendars on the Internet and have those calendar events included with the calendar you keep on your iPad. You'll find calendars everywhere and for almost anything, including for your favorite sports teams, for your kid's lunch program at school, for work-related holidays, and more. To find calendars, perform a Google search for iCal Calendars for iPad.

Chapter 9
Syncing, Backing Up, and Restoring

In this chapter you'll learn how to sync, back up, and restore your iPad. These are all important maintenance tasks. It's not something you do for fun, but it is what you do to keep your data secure and your iPad up-to-date.

Before we get started you should understand the basic terms we'll be using. Syncing is the act of transferring changes from your iPad to your computer and back again. Syncing keeps your iPad's data up-to-date and on the same page, so to speak, with your computer. Backing up is part of syncing, and is achieved each time you connect your iPad to your computer. However, you can encrypt (encode) your backups to further secure them, and back up your backups for even more peace of mind. Finally, restoring is the act of returning your iPad to some earlier state; this may include resetting

QUICKSTEPS

SYNCING ONLY SELECTED MUSIC

Connect your iPad to your computer and then complete the steps here to sync only specific music, artists, or playlists.

GETTING iTUNES READY TO SYNC SELECTED MUSIC

To get iTunes ready to sync selected music:

1. Click your iPad in the left pane.

2. Click the **Music** tab.

3. Verify that **Sync Music** is selected.

4. Click **Selected Playlists, Artists, Albums, And Genres**.

Summary	Info	Apps	**Music**

☑ **Sync Music**

○ Entire music library
◉ Selected playlists, artists, albums, and genres

SYNCING SPECIFIC MUSIC

To sync only specific music:

1. Under Playlists, select only the playlists you want to sync.

2. Under Artists, select only the artists you want to sync.

3. Under Genres, select only the artists you want to sync.

4. Under Albums, select only the albums you want to sync.

5. Click **Sync**.

Summary	Info	Apps	**Music**	Movies	TV Shows	Podcasts	iTunes U	Books

Playlists

- ☑ Purchased
- ☑ Purchased on Joli's iPad
- ▼ ☐ Genius Mixes
  - ☐ Contemporary Folk Mix
  - ☐ Blues, Boogie & Southern Rock Mix
- ☑ Music Videos
- ☑ Favorite Songs
- ☑ My Music
- ☑ Sleepy Time Music

Artists

- ☑ The Monkees
- ☑ Pink Floyd
- ☑ The Pretenders
- ☐ Richard Stoltzman
- ☐ Silver Mount Zion
- ☑ Simon & Garfunkel
- ☑ Sonny & Cher
- ☑ Tears for Fears
- ☑ Tom Petty & The Heartbreakers

the icons on the Home screen, resetting default settings, or returning your iPad to the state it was in when you first purchased it.

Configure Advanced Syncing

You've already learned in various chapters in this book how to sync your iPad to your computer. However, more advanced syncing techniques are available that have not yet been introduced. For the most part, those techniques involve only syncing the data you want to sync so that you have exactly what you want on your iPad and nothing more. In addition to syncing only specific media, like photos, videos, and music, you can opt to sync calendar events, contacts, apps, and books, among other things.

Manage Music

You learned a bit about syncing all of your media in Chapter 1. You learned how to select and sync only the pictures and videos you want on your iPad in Chapter 4. You even learned how to put music on your iPad by syncing with iTunes in Chapter 5. However, you may not have experimented with only syncing specific artists, albums, genres, playlists, and the like. Because you might have acquired quite a library of songs on your computer, it may be in your best interest to limit how much of that music syncs to your iPad.

NOTE

Before you can configure syncing, you must connect your iPad to your computer using the supplied USB cable. Wait while the iPad is backed up and then click the iPad in the left pane of iTunes (on your computer) to get started here.

NOTE

To replace all of the contacts on your iPad during the next sync only with the information on your computer, under Advanced, select **Contacts**.

Sync Contacts and Notes

You learned about the Contacts and Calendars apps in Chapter 8, and you learned how to create calendars on your computer and sync them to your iPad. You didn't learn how to sync Contacts or Notes, however, two additional items available for syncing. The way you sync your contacts depends on the e-mail program you use, the e-mail addresses you have configured, and other criteria. As you can see in Figure 9-1, you may have several options when configuring syncing. You'll have to decide which of your contact options you prefer. The way you sync any notes you create also depends on the programs you have installed on your computer.

To sync contact data:

1. With your iPad connected to your computer, in iTunes, select your iPad in the left pane.

2. Click the **Info** tab.

3. Select **Sync Contacts With**; then:

   a. Click the arrow next to **With** (see Figure 9-1).

   b. Select the e-mail program you use on your computer.

   c. Select **All Contacts** or another option, if applicable.

4. Select **Sync Notes With**; then:

   d. Click the arrow next to **With**.

   e. Select a compatible program you use on your computer.

	Summary	Info	Apps	Music	Movies	TV Shows	Podcasts	iTunes U	Books

MobileMe

Learn More   You can use MobileMe to sync your email, calendars, contacts, and bookmarks with your iPad.

☑ **Sync Contacts with** [Outlook ▾]
- ✓ Outlook
- Google Contacts
- Windows Contacts
- Yahoo! Address Book

◉ All contacts
◯ Selected group
   ☐ Collected

☐ Add contacts created outside of groups on this iPad to: [▾]

Figure 9-1: From the Info tab in iTunes, select which contacts you want to sync.

Other

☐ Sync bookmarks with [Internet Explorer ▾]
☑ Sync notes with [Outlook ▾]
   Your notes are being synced over the air. Your notes will also sync directly with this com your device

5. Click **Apply**.

SYNCING ONLY SPECIFIC APPS

When you acquire apps and then sync your iPad with your computer, those apps are backed up to the computer. If you decide you no longer want an app to appear on your iPad, you can tap and hold on any app, and then tap the X when it appears to remove it from your iPad. (Tap the Home button when finished.)

Alternately, in iTunes, you can opt not to sync an app. The app will still be available on your computer should you want it again, but it will not appear on your iPad. You decide what to sync and not sync from the Apps tab in iTunes when your iPad is connected to your computer and selected.

To sync only specific apps:

1. Connect your iPad to your computer, and in iTunes, select the iPad in the left pane.

2. Click the **Apps** tab.

3. Select **Sync Apps**.

4. Select the apps you want to sync.

5. Click **Apply**.

Sync Mail Accounts

You might be tempted to simply select the option to sync your mail accounts and assume that your e-mail messages, contacts, passwords, and the like would be synced after clicking Apply. That's not what syncing mail accounts is all about, and none of that actually happens. When you opt to sync mail accounts, what you're doing is syncing your account *settings*. These are things like your POP3 server names and your SMTP server names, your ports, and other technical data. If you set up your mail accounts in Chapter 3 and they're working properly, don't opt to sync these accounts. If you had problems in Chapter 3, you can try syncing your account settings here.

To sync mail account settings:

1. With your iPad connected to your computer, in iTunes, select your iPad in the left pane.

2. Click the **Info** tab.

3. Select **Sync Mail Accounts From**.

4. Select the e-mail program you use on your computer to obtain e-mail from the account (see Figure 9-2).

5. Click **Apply**.

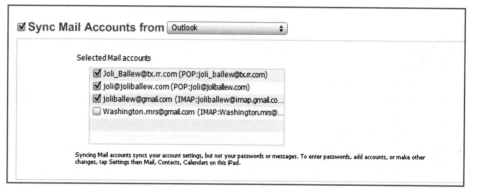

Figure 9-2: **You can sync e-mail account settings, but only do this if you could not set up your mail accounts manually.**

Sync Books

If you've purchased books from the iBookstore and read them, you may want to move them off of your iPad but keep them in case you want to read them again. You can do this from the Books tab of iTunes. Figure 9-3 shows this tab.

Figure 9-3: *The Books tab offers the ability to sync only specific books, such as those you've yet to read or want access to all the time.*

Back Up Your iPad

Backing up your iPad data is important, and you should back up your iPad regularly, especially after you acquire books, videos, music, or apps you've paid for, or take pictures or videos with the camera. Those purchases won't be backed up until you connect your iPad to your computer, and if they're lost, sometimes they're gone for good. Another reason is so that you have a backup in case your iPad is lost, stolen, or broken. You can use your latest backup to restore your iPad if you replace it with a new one.

When you connect your iPad to your computer, iTunes performs a simple backup. This backup includes your iPad's operating system, your apps, the settings you've configured, application data, and various other data that is directly related to the iPad. You can manually create a backup by connecting your iPad to your computer anytime.

To manually create a backup:

1. Connect your iPad to your computer.
2. Make sure your computer is connected to the Internet.
3. Right-click your iPad in the sidebar of iTunes.
4. Click **Backup**. Note you can also opt to transfer purchases.

Encrypt Your Backups

For extra security, you can set iTunes to encrypt your backups. When you encrypt your backups, you assign a password to them. You'll have to input the password to restore the data later, should you need to. This will keep others from accessing your backup and keep the backup more secure.

To encrypt your backup:

1. Connect your iPad to your computer.
2. In iTunes, select your iPad in the left pane.
3. Click the **Summary** tab.
4. Select **Encrypt iPad Backup**.

5. Type a password, type it again, and then click **Set Password**.

Back Up Your Backups

iPad backups, at least on PCs, are stored (and hidden away) in your User's folder. It's also likely that your music is stored in your Music folder, Videos in the Videos folder, Pictures in the Pictures folder, and so on. These are all subfolders of your User's folder. You can back up your iPad data as well as your personal data by backing up this personal folder. Macs perform and organize data similarly.

One way to back up your data is to use a backup program. Windows offers a program called Backup and Restore. The first time you run it, you'll be prompted to set it up. During the setup process, make sure that you back up your User's folder and, if available, create a system image. This will copy everything and save it to an external source, which will be a great help if something happens to the computer that holds your iPad backups and your iPad.

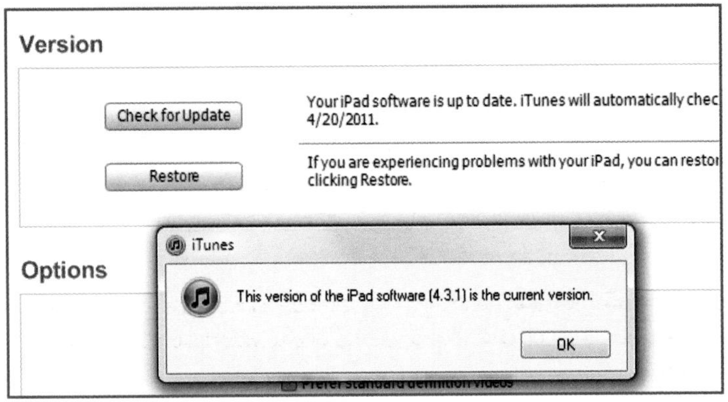

Figure 9-4: *Three or four times a year, manually check for iPad updates.*

Update Your iPad

Once in a while, Apple makes an update available for your iPad. These updates may include new features, security enhancements, or new settings or options. You can easily check for updates by connecting your iPad to your computer, and in iTunes, from the Summary tab, clicking **Check For Updates**. You'll likely see that your iPad is up-to-date, shown in Figure 9-4.

Restore or Reset Your iPad

You can restore your iPad from a backup if something happens to it or if you have to buy a new iPad. You can reset an existing iPad's settings to the default settings or to prepare an iPad for a new owner.

Restore from a Backup

If you've created a backup using iTunes, you have a copy of your settings, application data, your iPad's operating system, and various other pertinent data. And if you've synced your iPad with your computer, you have a backup of all of your media too. You can restore from these two backups should you ever need to. You can restore the data to your existing iPad, or, if the iPad was lost, stolen, or damaged, you can restore to a new iPad.

TIP

You also can check for updates to iTunes from the Help menu (Check For Updates).

TAKING ACTION WHEN YOUR iPAD IS "FROZEN"

If your iPad isn't responding and seems to be "frozen," you can try several things before you opt to reset or restore from a backup:

- If your screen won't rotate, verify that the screen rotation lock is not engaged. Likewise, if there's no sound, verify that the silent switch has not been applied.

- If an application seems to be the cause of the iPad's unresponsiveness, press and hold the **Sleep/Wake** button. When the red slider appears, let go of the **Sleep/Wake** button and then press and hold the **Home** button. This should close the current application. Your iPad may be just fine after that. Sometimes third-party apps are "buggy" and cause the iPad to freeze up. If you deem this to be the case, it's best to uninstall or delete the app.

- If the battery is low on power, charge the iPad by connecting it to a wall outlet using the power adapter. A low battery shouldn't cause the iPad to freeze up, but it might "go to sleep" while you're trying to use it.

- If the previous options don't work or are not the issue, you'll need to turn off the iPad and turn it back on. Press and hold the **Sleep/Wake** button, and when the red slider appears, drag the slider to turn off the iPad. Then press and hold the **Sleep/Wake** button again to turn the iPad back on.

- As a last resort, reset the iPad. Resetting won't cause data loss if you choose the right option; it's like rebooting a computer. Press and hold the **Sleep/Wake** button and the **Home** button simultaneously for ten seconds. When the Apple logo appears, let go. The iPad will reset.

To restore your iPad from a backup:

1. At the computer where you manage your iPad, connect to the Internet.

2. Connect your iPad to the computer.

3. In iTunes, right-click on a PC or **CTRL**-click on a Mac on the iPad in the sidebar, and then choose **Restore From Backup** from the context menu that appears.

4. Choose the backup that you want to restore from, and then click **Restore**. Use the drop-down menu to review your options. If the backup is encrypted, you'll need to enter your password.

5. Your iPad will restart. Leave it connected until it's finished.

Restore to Factory Settings

The only time you'll want to restore your iPad to factory settings is if you want to sell it, give it away, or completely start fresh. Restoring to factory settings will erase everything on your iPad, including your personal data, apps, books,

NOTE

If you don't want to restore your iPad to factory settings but only want to reset specific items (like the Home screen icons, keyboard dictionary, or network settings), skip to the next section.

TIP

You can connect your iPad to your computer, and from the Summary tab in iTunes, click **Restore**. This will also restore your iPad to factory settings.

TIP

You can call Apple at 1-800-My-Apple to ask for help if you need it. Don't restore your iPad to factory settings just because you're having trouble with it; give them a call first.

QUICKSTEPS

RESETTING YOUR HOME SCREEN LAYOUT

When you reset your Home screen layout, the default Home screen will be returned to its native configuration. Apps that are not supposed to be on the Home screen will be moved to other screens.

To reset your Home screen layout:

1. Tap **Settings**.
2. Tap **General**.
3. Scroll down and tap **Reset**.
4. Tap **Reset Home Screen Layout**.
5. If applicable, input your passcode.
6. Tap **Reset** to apply or **Cancel** to quit.

and any other data you've acquired (although it won't erase this data from your computer, should you be interested in, say, upgrading to an iPad 3 sometime in the future). Your settings, preferences, preferred networks, and everything else will be reset to the defaults. Restoring to factory settings makes the iPad look and act like it did the day you brought it home.

Now you're ready to restore your iPad to factory defaults.

1. From your iPad, tap **Settings**.
2. Tap **General**.
3. Tap **Reset**.
4. Tap **Erase All Content And Settings**.
5. Once the restore is complete, disconnect your iPad and do not sync it again.

Reset Your iPad

Using your iPad, you can reset the following:

- **Reset All Settings**   This will reset all settings (listed later), but will not delete any media or personal data.
- **Erase All Content And Settings**   Outlined in the previous section, this option returns the iPad to factory defaults and erases all personal data, apps, media, and personal settings.
- **Reset Network Settings**   This will delete all network settings, returning them to factory defaults.
- **Reset Keyboard Dictionary**   This will delete all custom words you have typed on the keyboard, returning the keyboard dictionary to factory defaults.
- **Reset Home Screen Layout**   This will reset your Home screen layout to factory defaults. The default Home screen layout is shown in Figure 9-5.
- **Reset Location Warnings**   This will reset your location warnings to factory defaults.

Figure 9-5: *This is the native Home screen layout.*

How to...

- *Use Airplane Mode*
- *Enable, Disable, and Manage Wi-Fi*
- *Joining a Different Wi-Fi Network*
- *Manage Notifications*
- *Configure Location Services*
- *Enable, Disable, and Manage Cellular Data*
- *Change Brightness and Wallpaper*
- *Configure Picture Frame*
- *Change General Settings*
- *Connecting a Bluetooth Device*
- *Set Defaults for Mail, Contacts, Calendars*
- *Changing Your Search Engine*
- *Set Defaults for Safari*
- *Configure Media Preferences*
- *Enabling Closed Captioning*
- *Set FaceTime Defaults*
- *Configuring Settings for Any Third-Party App*
- *Set Notes Defaults*
- *Set Store Defaults*
- *Manage Apps*

Chapter 10
Exploring Settings

Throughout this book, you've configured some settings for apps on your iPad. In Chapter 1 you used the Settings app to apply a passcode lock to protect your iPad; in Chapter 2 you enabled Wi-Fi and cellular data features so you could get online; in Chapter 3 you explored some of the available Mail settings like setting the font size for e-mail you receive—you get the idea. However, it's important to explore all of the options in the Settings app so that you can return here as needed and make configuration changes.

This chapter explains what's available in the Settings app. Configuring settings is generally a straightforward process, once you know where to find what you need.

Explore Settings

The Settings icon enables you to customize your iPad's apps and set preferences. This is where you'll go to change your wallpaper, configure settings for Safari, and configure preferences for Picture Frame, among other things. There's a wide range of settings to choose from and lots of preferences you can set. You can configure preferences and settings in the following categories:

- Airplane Mode
- Wi-Fi, Notifications
- Location Services
- Cellular Data (iPad 3G only)
- Brightness and Wallpaper
- Picture Frame
- General
- Mail, Contacts, Calendars
- Safari
- iPod
- Video
- Photos
- FaceTime
- Notes
- Store

NOTE

Each time you change a setting in the Settings app, the change is applied immediately. You do not have to tap **Save**, for example.

Although we've introduced some of these settings in this book, this chapter outlines what you can do within each category of settings. The chapter is organized by what you *can do* then; it is not simply a list of settings and how to enable or disable them (which was covered throughout this book).

Use Airplane Mode

When you are on an airplane, you'll often be advised when you can use "approved devices." The iPad is one of those approved devices, provided you disable the wireless features of the device. You may want to enable Airplane Mode to increase battery life when you know you won't be connecting to any networks as well. For more information about networks, see Chapter 2.

To enable Airplane Mode:

1. Tap **Settings**.

2. Tap the slider next to Airplane Mode (moving it from Off to On).

3. Tap again to turn off Airplane Mode.

Enable, Disable, and Manage Wi-Fi

You configure Wi-Fi settings to state how the iPad should use local Wi-Fi networks to connect to the Internet. You'll want to leave Wi-Fi enabled when you know you'll be accessing the Internet from your home network or a wireless hotspot. If no Wi-Fi networks are available, or if you turn Wi-Fi off, the iPad will connect to the Internet over your cellular data network (on iPad Wi-Fi + 3G only), if it's available and if you subscribe to a cellular data service. For more information about networks, see Chapter 2.

Wi-Fi options include the ability to:

- **Turn Wi-Fi on or off.**

- **Join a Wi-Fi network** You first select a network from the list, and then enter a password if necessary.

- **Set iPad to ask if you want to join available networks** This will notify you when networks are available (or not).

- **Forget a network so iPad doesn't join it automatically** You want to "forget" networks you know you'll never use, because your iPad works through all of the networks when looking for one. This uses battery power and takes time. It's best to keep the list short and only filled with networks you recognize. To do this, tap next to a network you've joined before, and then tap **Forget This Network**.

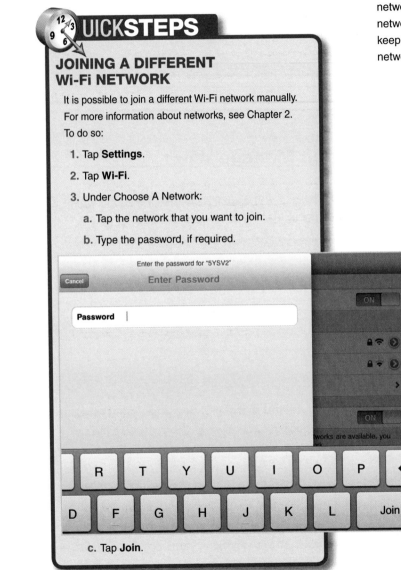

JOINING A DIFFERENT Wi-Fi NETWORK

It is possible to join a different Wi-Fi network manually. For more information about networks, see Chapter 2. To do so:

1. Tap **Settings**.

2. Tap **Wi-Fi**.

3. Under Choose A Network:

   a. Tap the network that you want to join.

   b. Type the password, if required.

   c. Tap **Join**.

Wi-Fi Networks	3802	
Forget this Network		

IP Address

DHCP	BootP	Static

IP Address		192.168.1.11
Subnet Mask		255.255.255.0
Router		192.168.1.1
DNS		192.168.1.1
Search Domains		
Client ID		

Renew Lease		

HTTP Proxy

Off	Manual	Auto

- **Join a closed Wi-Fi network** To join a Wi-Fi network that isn't shown in the list of networks, tap **Other** and then enter the network name and other required information, such as a password

- **Adjust settings to connect to a Wi-Fi network** Change settings for your current Wi-Fi network.

10

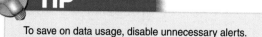

Manage Notifications

When you configure the Game Center or install certain third-party apps, you'll be asked to allow the app to send notifications to your iPad automatically. These notifications can include badges, alerts, and sounds. When enabled, apps can alert you about new information, even when the application isn't running. Most notifications play a sound, offer text, or place a number on the app's icon on the Home screen. For more information about using apps, see Chapter 6.

Notifications options include the ability to:

- **Turn all notifications on or off**.

- **Turn sounds, alerts, or badges on or off for an application**   These turn off notifications for a specific app. (Note that "badges" are the notifications that appear on an icon, such as the number of new Facebook status updates.) See Figure 10-1.

To turn off notifications for any app:

1. Tap **Settings**.

2. Tap **Notifications**.

3. Tap the arrow associated with the app you want to change.

4. In the resulting page, opt to turn off the notifications you do not want sent to you. This might include Sounds, Alerts, or Badges, for instance.

Notifications

Notifications   ON

Turn off Notifications to disable Sounds, Alerts and Home Screen Badges for the applications below.

Game Center
Badges, Alerts, Sounds   >

Ping
Badges, Alerts, Sounds   >

Figure 10-1: Apps that offer notifications will appear in the Notifications section of Settings.

Configure Location Services

Location Services is what enables an app, say Maps, the Camera, and other apps (including third-party apps), to determine your approximate location. You may want to disable this to maintain your privacy. However, most apps that want information regarding your location want it to make your experience with the app more valuable. For instance, when Location Services for Maps is enabled, you can tap the Location icon to

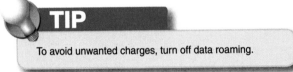

Location Services

| **Location Services** | ON |

Allow the apps below to determine your approximate location.

bing **Bing for iPad**	ON
◉ **Camera**	ON
Maps	✦ ON

An app that has requested your location within the last 24 hours will show the location services icon next to its name.

let Maps figure out where you are, perhaps to use as a starting point for directions you'd like to acquire. Third-party apps, such as Bing for iPad, shown here, use your location to offer information about the weather and local businesses, among other things.

Location Services includes the ability to:

- **Turn Location Services on or off** This enables or disables Location Services for all apps.
- **Turn Location Services on or off for specific apps** Turn on or off Location Services for only the apps you want.

Enable, Disable, and Manage Cellular Data

Cellular Data settings are available only on the iPad Wi-Fi + 3G model and are shown in Figure 10-2. They enable you to change settings related to your current cellular data network, and turn cellular data and/or roaming on or off. For more information about networks, see Chapter 2.

TIP

To avoid unwanted charges, turn off data roaming.

Cellular Data

| **Cellular Data** | ON |

| **Data Roaming** | OFF |

Turn data roaming off when abroad to avoid substantial roaming charges when using email, web browsing, and other data services.

| **View Account** |

View account information or add more data.

| **SIM PIN** | > |

Cellular Data options include the ability to:

- **Turn the cellular data network connection on or off** You may want to turn off cellular network access when you know you'll be away from Wi-Fi networks but also know you won't be needing Internet access.
- **Turn data roaming on or off** Data roaming may cost extra if you're out of the country. It's best to leave this off until you fully understand your plan.
- **View your account information** See or change your account information.
- **Add a SIM PIN** You can add a PIN to lock your micro-SIM card. If your iPad is stolen, a thief could possibly pull out the SIM card and obtain data from it.

Figure 10-2: Data Roaming should be turned off in almost all instances.

10

Change Brightness and Wallpaper

Use Brightness settings to adjust the screen brightness and wallpaper settings to personalize your iPad's Home screen wallpaper and the picture you see when you unlock your iPad. For more information about personalizing your iPad with wallpaper, see Chapter 1.

Brightness and Wallpaper options include the ability to:

- **Adjust the screen brightness**   You do this using a slider.
- **Set whether iPad adjusts screen brightness automatically**   Enable or disable Auto-Brightness. When Auto-Brightness is enabled, your iPad will adjust the brightness automatically using the built-in ambient light sensor.
- **Set wallpaper**   Select a wallpaper for the Lock screen, Home screen, or both. Figure 10-3 shows the available wallpapers.

Figure 10-3: The Brightness & Wallpaper settings let you apply new wallpaper to the Lock screen, Home screen, or both, and change the brightness.

Picture Frame

Picture Frame mode turns your iPad into an animated picture frame.

Transition

Dissolve	✓
Origami	

Show Each Photo For	3 Seconds ›
Zoom in on Faces	ON
Shuffle	OFF

All Photos	✓
Albums	
Events	

TIP

To enhance battery life, turn off Bluetooth when you aren't using it.

Configure Picture Frame

You can use your iPad as a digital picture frame. You can enhance this by also incorporating the optional dock to hold the frame in place on a mantle or table. Picture Frame mode lets you also apply transitions in between photos and choose what photos to display. You can even zoom in on faces and shuffle photos when playing them. For more information about sharing pictures, see Chapter 4.

Picture Frame options include the ability to:

- **Select a transition**   Choose the type of transition to use between photos.
- **Show a picture for a specific time**   Specify how long a picture should remain on the screen until it moves to the next one.
- **Zoom in on faces during a Picture Frame show**   This option only works when **Dissolve** is selected as the transition.
- **Shuffle**   Randomizes the order in which photos are displayed.
- **Choose what pictures to show**   Select a folder or all photos to use when Picture Frame is playing.

Change General Settings

General settings include those related to the date and time, security, network, and other things that affect every part of your iPad. This is also where you can find information about your iPad, or reset your iPad to its original state. The General settings offer subcategories, that, when selected, offer even more options. Listed next are the subcategories and what they include.

The General settings contain more options than any other feature in the Settings app. To use this:

1. Tap **Settings** on the Home screen.
2. Tap **General**.

3. Use your finger to scroll down so you can see every option.

4. If an option has an arrow by it, tap it to view the options available for it (see Figure 10-4).

5. Tap the **Back** button or tap **General** to return to the previous screen.

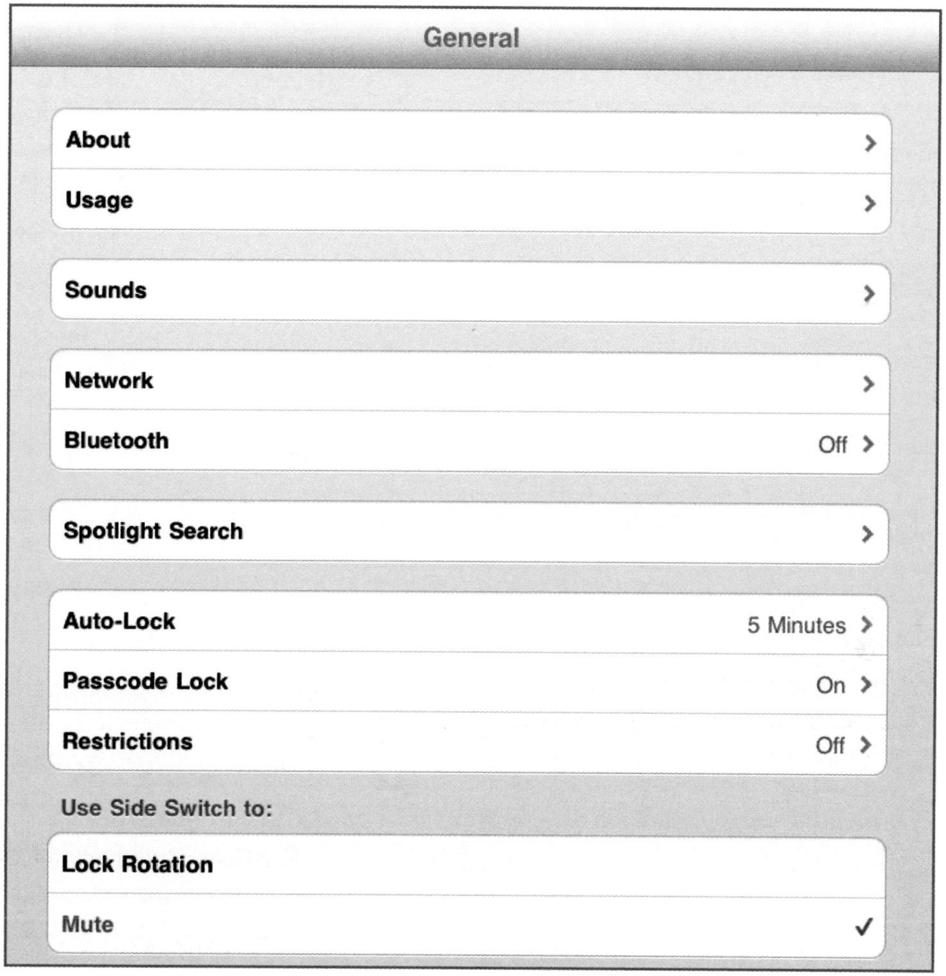

General	
About	>
Usage	>
Sounds	>
Network	>
Bluetooth	Off >
Spotlight Search	>
Auto-Lock	5 Minutes >
Passcode Lock	On >
Restrictions	Off >
Use Side Switch to:	
Lock Rotation	
Mute	✓

Figure 10-4: There are lots of options under the General setting.

10

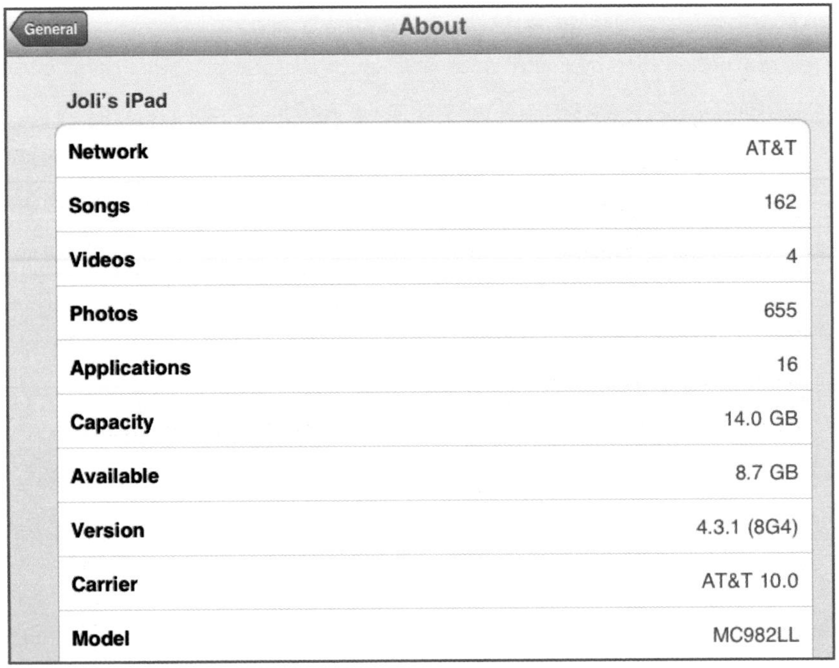

Figure 10-5: *As with other General options, tap General to return to the previous screen.*

ABOUT

Click About to get information about your iPad, including but not limited to, total storage capacity, space available, number of songs, videos, photos, serial number, and software version. See Figure 10-5.

USAGE

This setting is available on the iPad 3G model only. Click the Usage category to obtain information about your battery and the amount of cellular data you've sent and received. For more information about using cellular networks, refer to Chapter 2.

Usage options include the ability to:

- **Show battery percentage** Display the percentage of battery charge next to the battery icon on the Home screen. On iPad Wi-Fi models, this setting is available on the General settings menu, above the Reset option.

- **See cellular network data** View the amount of data sent and received over the cellular data network (on iPad Wi-Fi + 3G only) since the last time you reset your usage statistics.

- **Reset your usage statistics** Clear accumulated data and statistics.

SOUNDS

Click Sounds to make changes to settings related to sounds. For more information about personalizing your iPad, see Chapter 1.

Sounds options include the ability to:

- **Adjust the ringer and alerts volume**.

- **Set alert and effects sounds** Turn specific sounds on or off. You can enable or disable sounds for the following:
  - Alarm ringtones
  - Incoming e-mail messages
  - Sent e-mail messages

- Alerts for events
- Locking the iPad
- Typing using the keyboard

To make these changes:

1. In the Settings app, tap **General**.

2. Tap the arrow next to **Sounds**.

3. Tap the arrow next to **Ringtone** to change it, and then:

    a. Tap a new ringtone from the list.

    b. Tap **Sounds** (the Back button).

4. Tap the **On** button on any other line shown under Ringtone to turn that sound off.

Ringtone	Marimba >
New Mail	ON
Sent Mail	ON
Calendar Alerts	ON
Lock Sounds	ON
Keyboard Clicks	ON

NETWORK

Network settings enable you to access and change settings related to the various networks you use, including Wi-Fi and virtual private networks (VPNs). VPNs offer secure connections to networks using the Internet. For more information about networks, see Chapter 2.

Network options include the ability to:

- **Add a new VPN configuration** You'll have to drill down into VPN settings to access this command.

- **Change a VPN configuration**.
- **Turn VPN on or off**.
- **Delete a VPN configuration**.
- **Access Wi-Fi Settings**   These are the Wi-Fi settings detailed earlier.

BLUETOOTH

Your iPad can connect to Bluetooth devices like headphones and keyboards. Bluetooth devices allow you to listen or type without wires. There are three options for Bluetooth:

- **Turn Bluetooth on or off**.
- **Search for Bluetooth devices**   Watch while your iPad searches for Bluetooth devices, once Bluetooth is enabled.
- **Connect to a Bluetooth device**   Pair your iPad with a Bluetooth device in range. You first select a device from the list, and then you may be required to enter a password.

SPOTLIGHT SEARCH

When you search with Spotlight, the iPad searches through the data on it to find what you need. You can state which data Spotlight Search should consider. You can choose to enable or disable Audiobooks, Contacts, Applications, Music, Podcasts, Videos, Notes, Mail, and Events. You can also drag any item to the top of the list or the bottom, to have it searched first or last, or in any order desired. The only option here is to tell Spotlight Search what data to look through.

AUTO-LOCK

Locking the iPad turns the display off. There's a button on the outside of your iPad for locking it. You can turn the display off to maximize battery life, but it will lock itself after a few minutes of idle time anyway. Locking the iPad also keeps it safe from unintended operation by preventing taps on the screen from activating an app. You can also require a passcode when you're ready to unlock your iPad. Passcode features are not enabled by default. By setting a passcode, you can prevent your iPad from being accessed without your permission, detailed in the next section. To enable Auto-Lock and Passcode

---

UICKSTEPS

CONNECTING A BLUETOOTH DEVICE

A compatible Bluetooth device is a wireless device you can use with your iPad, such as a wireless headset, wireless speakers, or wireless keyboard. You must "pair" the device with your iPad. Pairing allows the device and the iPad to agree on a Bluetooth frequency so that they can communicate effectively without "crossing signals" with any other Bluetooth devices you may have installed.

To connect a Bluetooth device:

1. Turn on your new Bluetooth device, insert batteries, or perform any other step to power on the device.
2. Follow the directions for the device to make it discoverable.
3. Locate and tap the **Settings** icon on the Home screen.
4. Tap **General**.
5. Tap **Bluetooth** and move the slider to **On**.
6. Wait while the iPad searches for Bluetooth devices.
7. When it finds the device, type the device's passkey or PIN when prompted.
8. To turn off Bluetooth, again tap **Settings**, then tap **General**, tap **Bluetooth**, and move the virtual switch to the **Off** position.

2 Minutes	✓
5 Minutes	
10 Minutes	
15 Minutes	
Never	

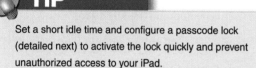

TIP

Set a short idle time and configure a passcode lock (detailed next) to activate the lock quickly and prevent unauthorized access to your iPad.

Lock, see Chapter 1. The only options here are to set the amount of time before the iPad locks or to disable Auto-Lock.

PASSCODE LOCK

You can secure your iPad by requiring a passcode lock. When you enable this feature, each time you unlock your iPad, you have to input this code. This keeps it safe from unauthorized users. To enable Auto-Lock and Passcode Lock, see Chapter 1.

Passcode Lock options include the ability to:

- **Set a passcode** Enter a four-digit passcode.
- **Turn Passcode Lock off**.
- **Change the passcode**.
- **Set how long before your passcode is required** Set how long the iPad should be idle before you need to enter a passcode to unlock it.
- **Picture frame** Determine whether to require a passcode (or not) when showing pictures with Picture Frame.
- **Erase data after 10 failed passcode attempts** If you turn on this feature, after 10 failed passcode attempts the iPad erases all your information and media.

RESTRICTIONS

Restrictions on the iPad are kind of like parental controls on other devices. You can set restrictions for iPod content on the iPad, as well as a few other applications like YouTube or iTunes.

Restriction options include the ability to:

- **Enable restrictions** You'll have to create and enter a four-digit passcode.
- **Turn off restrictions**.
- **Set application restrictions** Set restrictions on individual apps, including Safari, YouTube, Camera, FaceTime, iTunes, Ping, Installing Apps, and Deleting Apps. You can also allow or disallow changes to Location and Accounts.

Restrictions

General

Disable Restrictions

Allow:

Safari		ON
YouTube		ON
Camera		ON
FaceTime		ON
iTunes		ON
Ping		ON
Installing Apps		ON
Deleting Apps		ON

- **Set allowed content**   Set restrictions on the type of content that can be played with regard to ratings. These include in-app purchases, ratings for a specific country, music and podcasts, movies, TV shows, apps, and Game Center's multiplayer games as well as the ability to add friends.

SIDE SWITCH

Here you configure what you want the side switch to do. It can be a lock rotation or it can mute the iPad.

DATE AND TIME

Settings are available to personalize the date and time information on your iPad.

These options include the ability to:

- **Set whether iPad shows 24-hour time or 12-hour time**.
- **Set Automatically**   With this feature activated, the iPad sets the time automatically. If it is turned off, you can manually set a time zone as well as a date and time.

KEYBOARD

You can change various settings for the keyboard and set preferences for how you type. For instance, you can turn on or off the Auto-Capitalization feature if you'd rather not have the iPad automatically capitalize the beginning of sentences (see Figure 10-6).

Keyboard options include the ability to:

- **Turn Auto-Correction on or off**.
- **Turn Auto-Capitalization on or off**.
- **Check Spelling**.

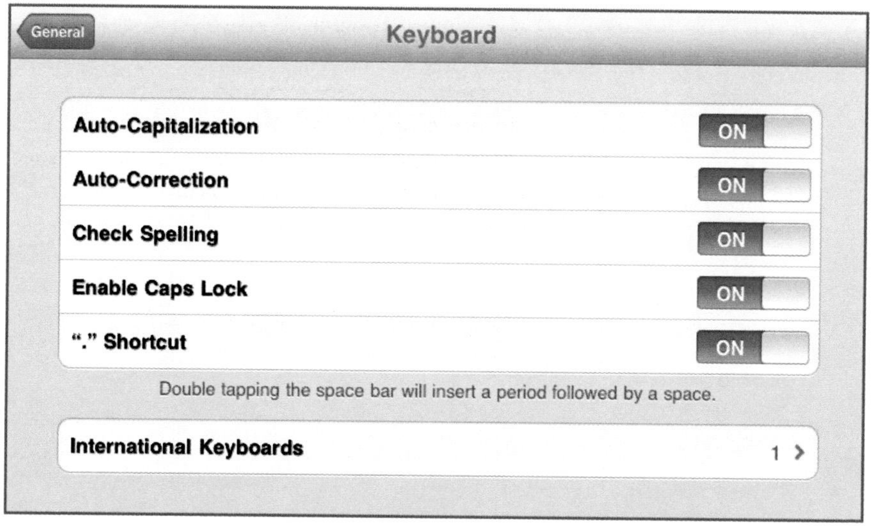

Figure 10-6: As with other settings, simply tap to turn a feature on or off.

- **Set whether the Caps Lock feature is enabled** Enabling this setting lets you double-tap the **SHIFT** key to engage Caps Lock mode. If disabled, a double-tap does not engage Caps Lock mode.

- **Turn the "." shortcut on or off** The "." shortcut lets you double-tap the **SPACEBAR** to enter a period followed by a space when you're typing.

- **Set up international keyboards** Add and configure keyboards for multiple languages.

INTERNATIONAL

Your iPad comes with various international settings. With these, you can set the language for the iPad, turn keyboards for different languages on or off, and configure similar preferences for your preferred language.

International options include the ability to:

- **Set the language for the iPad**.
- **Set up international keyboards**.
- **Set date, time, and telephone number formats for your specific region**.
- **Set calendar** You can currently choose from Gregorian, Japanese, and Buddhist.

ACCESSIBILITY

Accessibility options make it easier for a person with a visual, mobility, or hearing disability to use the iPad.

Accessibility options include the ability to:

- **Have what's on your iPad's screen read to you using VoiceOver**.
- **Zoom in on your iPad's screen**.
- **Use large text** This makes text larger in Contacts, Mail, and Notes.
- **Use a high-contrast screen** This uses the white-on-black screen mode.
- **Use mono audio** Combine stereo audio channels so that identical sound is heard in both.

- **Speak Auto-text** Have the iPad speak auto-corrections and auto-capitalizations to you.
- **Triple-click Home** This allows you to triple-click the Home button to toggle some accessibility features.

RESETTING iPAD

You will change the default values for various settings on your iPad as you use it. You'll likely reorder the Home screen, add words to the Dictionary while typing, or change Network settings. You can reset these by resetting specific apps on your iPad. You can also reset your iPad and delete everything on it, restoring it to factory settings.

Resetting iPad options include the ability to:

- **Reset all settings** This only applies to settings on the iPad, not your data (like contacts, calendars, and media).
- **Erase all content and settings** This completely resets your iPad and deletes all of the data on it.
- **Reset network settings**.
- **Reset the keyboard dictionary**.
- **Reset the Home screen layout**.
- **Reset the location warnings**.

TIP

Before you sell, trade, give, or donate your iPad, erase all content and settings.

Mail, Contacts, Calendars	
Accounts	
MobileMe Find My iPad	>
Joli_Ballew@tx.rr.com Mail	>
joli@joliballew.com Mail	>
joliballew@gmail.com Mail, Notes	>
Subscribed Calendars UK Holidays	>
Add Account...	>
Fetch New Data	Push >
Mail	
Show	25 Recent Messages >
Preview	2 Lines >

Figure 10-7: As with other apps, arrows indicate that several options are available for a setting.

Set Defaults for Mail, Contacts, Calendars

You'll use the Mail, Contacts, Calendars settings to set up e-mail accounts and MobileMe. You can also customize preferences for these accounts and related features, including Contacts and Calendar. For more information about setting up Mail, see Chapter 3. For more information about the Contacts and Calendar apps, refer to Chapter 8.

To use the Mail, Contacts, Calendars options:

1. In the Settings app, tap **Mail, Contacts, Calendars**.
2. Scroll through the options in the right pane to explore them.
3. If an option has an arrow by it, tap the arrow to access the options.
4. Tap any option to change it. Figure 10-7 shows the Mail, Contacts, Calendars screen.

ACCOUNTS

This is where you configure the e-mail accounts and calendar subscriptions on your iPad. You can change your account settings, stop using an account, or even delete an account.

Account options include the ability to:

- **Change an account's settings** Choose an existing account and make changes to it.
- **Stop using an account** Disable an account.
- **Adjust advanced settings** For e-mail accounts, configure options such as mailbox behaviors and settings for incoming messages.
- **Delete an account from iPad** This deletes an account completely. If you want to use the account again, you'll have to reenter it. If you aren't sure, disable the account instead.

FETCH NEW DATA

Fetch and Push are two ways to obtain your e-mail. Push is a technology that allows Internet servers to send information to your iPad as soon as the message is received by your e-mail provider on their e-mail servers. Some e-mail servers will push e-mail to you, while others won't. Be aware that using Push will use battery power to obtain updates and transfer data, and can minimize battery life. Transfers while connected via 3G are counted toward your monthly data usage as well. This isn't a problem if you have a generous 3G data plan, but it can be if you have a limited plan.

Other e-mail accounts such as POP, IMAP, AOL, and Gmail accounts aren't Push-compatible on the iPad. This means that no e-mail will arrive at your Inbox in Mail until you open Mail and access the Inbox. At that time, Mail will check for e-mail and obtain it from your e-mail servers. If this is inconvenient and you'd rather have Mail check for e-mail automatically, even when you aren't using it, you can configure your iPad to fetch your e-mail on a schedule, such as every 15, 30, or 60 minutes. You can also set Fetch settings to Manually so that no fetch occurs by default. As with Push, Fetch will drain your battery more quickly on than off. To maximize battery life, fetch less often or fetch manually. Fetch also kicks in for Push e-mail accounts if Push is turned off, so if you're watching your data usage, you may need to turn off Push and set Fetch to Manually.

Fetch options include the ability to:

- **Turn Push on**.
- **Set the interval to fetch data**.

MAIL

You can configure lots of Mail settings. You can add a signature to all outgoing e-mails, set the minimum font size for e-mail messages, set a default e-mail account, and more.

TIP

To change the sounds associated with Mail, in Settings, go to the General options, under Sounds.

10

Mail options include the ability to:

- **Set the number of messages shown on the iPad**   You can opt to see the most recent 25, 50, 75, 100, or 200 messages.

- **Set how many lines of each message are previewed in the message list**   Change e-mail preview options, specifically, how many lines of text you'd like to preview (up to five).

- **Set a minimum font size for messages**   Set a font size, including Small, Medium, Large, Extra Large, or Giant.

- **Set whether iPad shows To and Cc labels in message lists**.

- **Set whether iPad confirms that you want to delete a message**.

- **Set whether iPad automatically loads remote images**   Loading remote images will cause the e-mail to take longer to load. You can manually load the images while reading the e-mail should you want to see them.

- **Organize by thread**   Have the iPad organize your e-mails by thread (conversation). A thread is created when you send e-mails back and forth to a person and the subject line remains the same.

Brightness & Wallpaper	**Preview** — 2 Lines >
Picture Frame	**Minimum Font Size** — Medium >
General	**Show To/Cc Label** — OFF
Mail, Contacts, Calendars	**Ask Before Deleting** — OFF
Safari	**Load Remote Images** — ON
iPod	**Organize By Thread** — ON
Video	**Always Bcc Myself** — OFF
Photos	**Signature** — Sent from my iPad >
FaceTime	**Default Account** — Joli_Ballew@tx.rr.com >
Notes	Messages created outside of Mail will be sent from the default account.

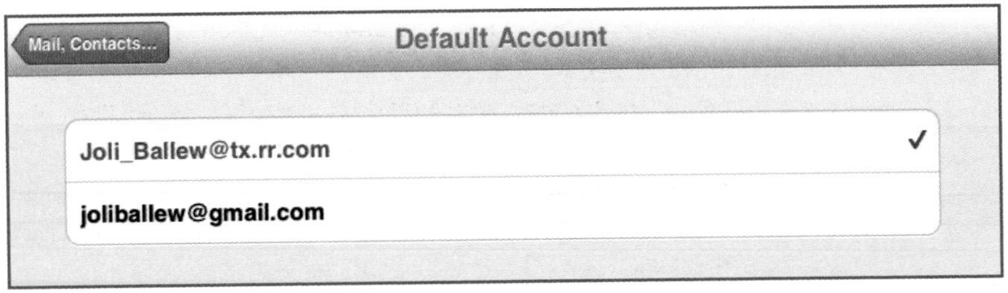

Default Account

Mail, Contacts...

Joli_Ballew@tx.rr.com ✓

joliballew@gmail.com

Figure 10-8: If you have more than one e-mail account, configure one as the default.

- **Set whether iPad sends you a copy of every message you send**   Send a blind carbon copy (Bcc) to yourself each time you send an e-mail.

- **Add a signature to your messages**   Add, change, or delete the automatic signature for outgoing messages.

- **Set the default e-mail account**   The default account is the one that will be used automatically each time you compose an e-mail (see Figure 10-8).

To set an e-mail account as the default:

1. In the Settings app, tap **Mail, Contacts, Calendars**.

2. Scroll down and tap the arrow by **Default Account**.

3. Tap the account you want to use as the default, shown in Figure 10-8.

CONTACTS

You can change how your contacts are sorted and displayed. For both, your choices are First, Last or Last, First.

CALENDAR

The Calendar helps you keep track of appointments and important dates. You can change how the Calendar sends you alerts, among other options.

To change the Calendar settings:

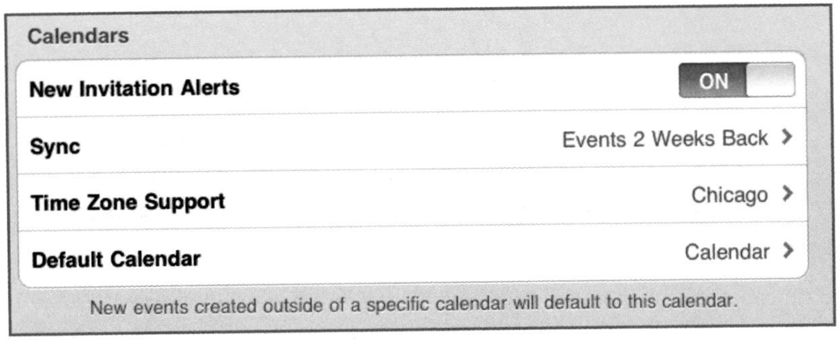

Calendars

New Invitation Alerts	ON
Sync	Events 2 Weeks Back >
Time Zone Support	Chicago >
Default Calendar	Calendar >

New events created outside of a specific calendar will default to this calendar.

Figure 10-9: Calendar options are at the bottom of the Mail, Contacts, Calendars page.

1. In the Settings app, tap **Mail, Contacts, Calendars**.

2. Scroll down to the **Calendars** section.

3. Tap to turn new invitation alerts on or off.

4. Tap the arrows by **Sync**, **Time Zone Support**, and **Default Calendar** to see additional options and apply them (see Figure 10-9).

Calendar options include the ability to:

- **Set alerts to sound when you receive meeting invitations**.

- **Set how far back in the past to show your calendar events on iPad**.

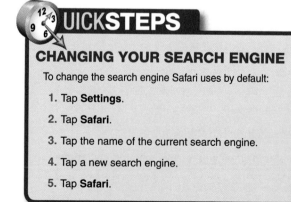

Safari

General

| Search Engine | Google > |

| AutoFill | Off > |

| Always Show Bookmarks Bar | ON |

Security

| Fraud Warning | ON |

Warn when visiting fraudulent websites.

- **Turn on Calendar time zone support** When enabled, the Calendar always displays your event dates and times using a specific time zone. When turned off, event dates and times are determined by the time zone of your current location.

- **Choose a default calendar** If you have more than one calendar configured on your iPad, you can set which of them is the default here.

Set Defaults for Safari

There are a few things you can configure regarding Safari. You can choose a specific search engine, enable AutoFill, always show the Bookmarks Bar, and change security settings. There are also "Developer" settings that you can likely ignore. For more information on using Safari, see Chapter 2.

GENERAL

General options include the ability to:

- **Select a search engine** Options include Google, Bing, and Yahoo!
- **Enable AutoFill** Set Safari to automatically fill out web forms. Safari remembers data you've previously entered into webpages for its data.
- **Show the Bookmarks Bar** When turned off, you can still reveal the Bookmarks Bar by clicking Safari's address bar or search box.

SECURITY

Security options include the ability to:

- **Change security settings** Turn Fraud Warning on or off; enable or disable JavaScript; block or allow pop-ups; set whether Safari accepts cookies; clear the history of webpages you've visited; clear all cookies from Safari; clear Safari's cache.

DEVELOPER

If you want to know when a webpage has errors, and if you're interested in resolving those errors because you develop apps or websites for the iPad, the debug console can help when this feature is turned on.

QUICKSTEPS

CHANGING YOUR SEARCH ENGINE

To change the search engine Safari uses by default:

1. Tap **Settings**.
2. Tap **Safari**.
3. Tap the name of the current search engine.
4. Tap a new search engine.
5. Tap **Safari**.

Configure Media Preferences

Media consists of music, videos, and photos. The Settings app offers three options for dealing with these: iPod, Videos, and Photos.

CONFIGURE iPOD PREFERENCES

The iPod app is the app you use to play music. You can configure various settings for the iPod, including playing all songs at the same sound level and setting a volume limit, among other things. Some of these options must be made at your computer. For more information about using the iPod app, see Chapter 5.

iPod	
Sound Check	OFF
EQ	Off >
Volume Limit	Off >
Lyrics & Podcast Info	ON
Home Sharing	
Apple ID joli_ballew@tx.rr.com	
Password ••••••••	

An Apple ID is required to use Home Sharing.

iPod options include the ability to:

- **Set the iPod to play songs at the same sound level**   This enables Sound Check.
- **Use EQ to customize the sound**   Select an equalizer from a list of predefined settings.
- **Set a volume limit**   Set the maximum volume for the iPod and lock it, if desired.
- **Display song lyrics and information about podcasts (when applicable).**
- **Home Sharing**   You set up Home Sharing using your Apple ID and password. You'll need to enable Home Sharing in the same manner on your other i-devices, and you

can include up to five devices in any Home Sharing situation. Sharing will occur over your home Wi-Fi network, and you can then stream media from one device to another.

ENABLING CLOSED CAPTIONING

Closed captioning, when available, enables you to read the dialogue in a movie, TV show, or other media. To enable closed captioning:

1. Tap **Settings**.

2. Tap **Video**.

3. Move the slider for Closed Captioning to **On**.

CONFIGURE VIDEO PREFERENCES

Video settings offer options that apply to all video content, including rented movies. Some of the things you can configure include closed captioning and widescreen. For more information about using the Video app, refer to Chapter 4.

Video	
Start Playing	Where Left Off >
Closed Captioning	OFF
TV Out	
Widescreen	OFF
TV Signal	NTSC >

Video options include:

- **Set where to resume playing**   You can resume playing from the beginning or where you left off.

- **Turn closed captioning on or off**.

- **Turn widescreen on or off**   Turn this on to preserve the widescreen aspect ratio when watching a video made specifically for the wide screen.

- **Set the TV output signal to NTSC or PAL**   If you're using the iPad with a video output accessory, use this setting to determine what video format you'll output. If you're in the United States, NTSC is the correct choice. Elsewhere, try PAL.

CONFIGURE PHOTOS PREFERENCES

The settings in Photos are related only to slideshows. For more information about using the Photos app, refer to Chapter 4.

Photos options include:

- **Set the length of time each slide is shown**   Specify the length of time each photo in a slideshow should appear before the next photo appears.
- **Set whether to repeat slideshows once they are completed**.
- **Set photos to appear randomly or in order**.

Set FaceTime Defaults

You'll use the FaceTime options to enable or disable FaceTime and to configure the account you want to use and the e-mail associated with your account. You can also add another e-mail account if desired. There are only a couple of options, shown in Figure 10-10.

To change FaceTime settings:

1. In the Settings app, tap **FaceTime**.
2. To enable or disable FaceTime, tap **On** or **Off**, respectively (see Figure 10-10).
3. To add another e-mail address where you can be reached via FaceTime, tap **Add Another Email**, and fill out the information required.

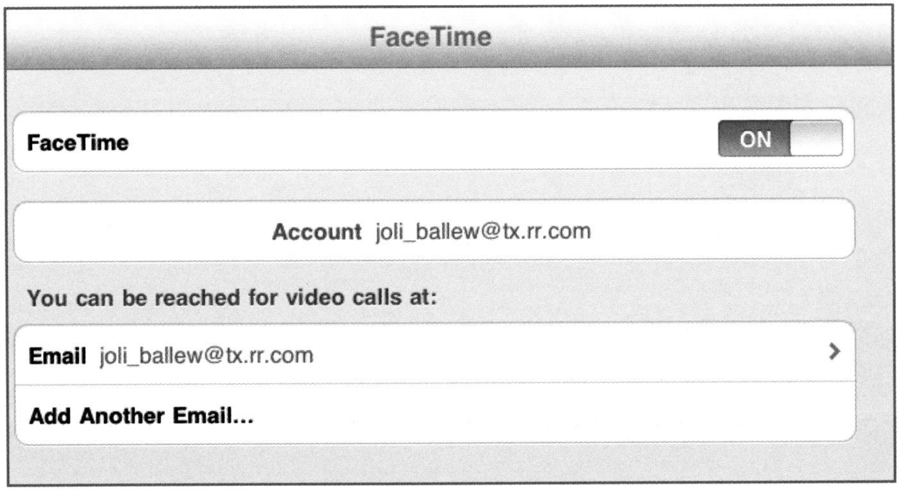

FaceTime
FaceTime ON
Account joli_ballew@tx.rr.com
You can be reached for video calls at:
Email joli_ballew@tx.rr.com >
Add Another Email...

Figure 10-10: FaceTime can be enabled or disabled from Settings.

iBooks

iBooks 1.2.1 (335)

Full Justification	ON
Auto-hyphenation	ON

Auto-hyphenation requires iOS 4.2

Tap Left Margin	Previous Page >
Sync Bookmarks	ON
Sync Collections	ON

Copyright © 2011 Apple Inc. All rights reserved.

Set Notes Defaults

Tap any font to change the default font used for Notes. There are three: Noteworthy, Helvetica, and Market Felt. To create a note, tap **Notes** on the Home screen, and tap to begin typing. Notes will be saved automatically, and will appear in the left pane when in landscape view. Controls appear at the bottom of the screen.

Set Store Defaults

The Store settings offer a place to change or create an iTunes Store account. For more information about shopping iTunes, using the App Store, and making purchases from the iBookstore, refer to Chapter 6. You can only sign in or out of an account and view your personal Store information, such as your billing address and payment information.

Manage Apps

Apps you've acquired that offer settings options appear under the Apps section. What you see here will be specific to your iPad. Tap any app in the list to view the settings available. For more information about obtaining and using apps, refer to Chapter 6.

Index

References to figures are in italics.

browsing music, 73–74
configuring preferences, 160–161
controls, 74–75
libraries and categories, 74
Music library, 73
Music Videos library, 73
playing and controlling audio, 75–76
playlists, 75–79
Podcasts library, 73
Purchased and Purchased libraries, 73
Repeat button, 79
searching, 76
Shuffle option, 79
switching views, 75, 76
iTunes, 10, 82
authorizing an existing account, 4
Books tab, 131–132
browsing and buying movies, 86–87
browsing and buying music, 85–86
choosing a media category, 82–84
configuring, 6
creating a new iTunes Store account, 3
getting ready to sync selected music, 128
importing songs from a CD, 70
installing, 2–3
interface, 82–85
iTunes U tab, 88
narrowing down category results, 84–85
obtaining podcasts, 87
obtaining TV shows and audiobooks, 88
opening, 3
renting movies, 87
syncing audiobooks, 71–72
syncing e-mail accounts using iTunes,
    38–39
syncing personal music files, 70–71
syncing podcasts, 72
iTunes Store, settings, 163

J

jiggling icons, 13

K

keyboard
    settings, 152–153
    See also virtual keyboard

L

links, tapping, 28
Location Services, 143–144
Lock screen, 9
locking
    Auto-Lock, 17, *18*, 150–151
    Passcode Lock, 17, *18*, 151
    Screen Rotation Lock, 7–8
    Simple Passcode, 17
    sounds, 17

M

Mail, 11
    adding a MobileMe, Gmail, Yahoo!, or AOL
        account, 39–40
    adding another account type, 40–41
    composing new e-mail, 44–45
    configuring settings, 50, 155–159
    e-mailing multiple photos, 45–46
    Mailboxes view, 41
    opening attachments, 47–49
    personalizing Mail, 50–52
    reading e-mail, 42–43
    reading e-mail on multiple devices, 42
    responding to e-mail, 45
    searching for an e-mail, 49

sending a test e-mail, 45–47
sending an e-mail, 120
sending videos, 48
sounds, 16
syncing mail accounts, 130–131
syncing mail accounts using iTunes, 38–39
using gestures to manage e-mail, 46–47
viewing in landscape view, 44
Mail, Contacts, Calendars options, 155–159
Maps app, 10, 105, *106*
    dog ear feature, 108
    exploring Street View, 109–110
    finding your present location, 105–108
    getting a map to a contact's address, 119
    getting directions, 108–109
    marking a location, 109
    sharing a location, 109
    toolbar, 107
media, viewing in Safari, 30, 31
microphone, 7
Micro-SIM card tray, 9
MobileMe, 18
    adding an account, 39–40
    configuring settings, 155–159
    See also Mail
movies
    browsing and buying, 86–87
    playing, 64
    renting, 87
    streaming a movie to your television, 66
    See also Videos app
Movies tab, syncing, 5–6
music, 70
    browsing and buying, 73–74, 85–86
    creating a Genius playlist, 76–78
    creating a standard playlist, 77
    dragging and dropping, 70
    editing a playlist, 78

WiFi, 20–21, 24
    configuring settings, 141–142
    connecting to a WiFi network, 24–25
    enabling, 26
    joining a different WiFi network, 142
    roaming, 25
WiFi + 3G, 20–21, 24
    configuring Cellular Data settings, 144
    enabling cellular data, 26
    monitoring cellular data usage, 25–27

Y

Yahoo!
    adding an account, 39–40
    See also Mail
YouTube, 10, 101–102, *103*
    playing YouTube videos, 102
    rating and commenting on videos, 104
    searching, 102
    sharing videos, 104–105

switching between modes, 102
uploading your own video, 104–105

Z

zooming
    double-tapping to zoom, 14
    pinching to zoom in or out, 13
    in Safari, 31–32